Pitcairn Island
via the Panama Canal
in the 1920s

SS REMUERA'S VISITS TO THE
TINY PACIFIC ISLAND

DAVID RANSOM
FOREWORD BY GARRY LAW

One-o-Clock

First edition, published in 2021
ISBN 979 8 7030915 9 3

About the author

David Ransom was born in Brighton, UK. He served an apprenticeship as a compositor in the days of hot metal printing, before moving on to Apple computers and magazine design.

David has always had a fascination with history and has a varied collection of miscellaneous items related to Pitcairn Island, the New Zealand Shipping Company, and the history of photography. Occasionally some of these areas come together, and it is as a result of these fortunate links, together with his interest in genealogy, that he researches and writes articles, and self-publishes small books.

Currently editor of *The Bounty*, magazine of the Pitcairn and Norfolk Islands Society, he has previously edited *SERIAC News*, the magazine of the South East Region of the Institute of Amateur Cinematographers.

His other interests include the history of photography, robotics, family history research and pretending that he is learning all about Raspberry Pi computing.

Also by David Ransom

The Bounty Postcard Catalogue

X8 – Early New Zealand Shipping Company Postcards and their Photographers

Notes on Voyage, 1911 by John Lynn (edited by David Ransom)

Zeppelin Letters: London during the First World War

Ransom's Pitcairn Postcard Catalogue

The free guide to Postcard Backs

Pitcairn Postcard Magazine (published between 1998 and 2010)

Publications are available through Amazon, or from this website:
www.printerspie.co.uk

Table of contents

Foreword by Garry Law, SS *Remuera* researcher and historian 4

Preface 7

Introduction 8

Timeline of the 1920s 10

1920s – Steaming by Coal or Oil? 15

1921 – Travels Abroad – by an Aucklander 19

1921 – Visit to Pitcairn Island, 1st October 32

1922 – *Remuera* Repaired 35

1923 – *Remuera* Arrives, 29th January 39

1923 – N.Z. Naval Station 42

1923 – Pitcairn Island, 16th June 49

1923 – Lonely Pitcairn, 26th June 51

1923 – Pitcairn Island Lecture, 13th July 56

1923 – A fascinating diary 59

1923 – Pitcairners Visit London 111

1923 – Seeing London, 27th October 115

1924 – Island of Dreams, 7th and 14th June 119

1924 – All Blacks Depart, 30th July 139

1925 – A letter from Pitcairn 142

1925 – Pitcairn Island, an interesting narrative, 23rd March 143

1925 – The All Blacks, 4th April 146

1926-27 – Impromptu Ocean Race, 6th January 149

1927 – Sad times in the Old Country, 19th January 151

1929 – Girl injured at Pitcairn Island, 2nd January 155

1929 – Retirement of Captain James John Cameron 156

The photographers of Pitcairn and the Panama Canal 159

Rhymes en route – a passenger's poetry 167

Foreword

GARRY LAW

Robert Law on *Remuera*, 1931

My father Robert Law and his two younger brothers emigrated on the *Remuera* in 1931, with New Zealand Government assistance. They had recently lost their mother and their father lies at Ypres. My father was aged 19. In depression times there were few passengers, and the crew I think gave up on keeping lively Scots boys out of the first class passengers' pool. Young people on cruises? – yes there was a shipboard romance but Agnes from Kansas disembarked at Panama and a correspondence petered out. There was a Pitcairn stop and my father remembered trading a bowler hat for a bunch of bananas.

SS *Remuera* (1911-1940) was one of many ships that shaped the 20th century, expanding trade and taking migrants to new worlds. In a century of two calamitous wars she was a troop ship in the first and sunk in the second. Her owner, the New Zealand Shipping Company, had a long series of mixed cargo and passenger vessels all with Maori names starting with 'R'. Why *Remuera* in particular? – well it was a prestigious Auckland address when the ship was launched and this seems to have been the necessary association. Indeed it was where my parents lived late in life.

Maori trace their ancestry back to the canoes (waka) that brought their ancestors to New Zealand. Remuera is the waka of the Law family, as no doubt it is of many others.

With the family association I started a web page about the ship **www.lawas.co.nz/info/remuera/index.htm** Through that I came into contact with David and we have exchanged information for many years, though we have yet to meet in person! I was delighted when he asked me to write this foreword. His collections of words and pictures from the 1920s are evocative of the time and particularly of the attitudes of the period. His attention to detail is diligent and I know much of the information here was gleaned by patient research over years. Something here for all of Pitcairn enthusiasts, Panama Canal travellers, postcard collectors, photographers and maritime history buffs.

Enjoy!

Garry Law, Auckland, New Zealand

An early real photo postcard of the *Remuera*

Preface

I have been collecting and researching photographs and postcards of the New Zealand Shipping Company, together with those of Pitcairn Island, for a number of years. After my collection grew, I thought it would be a good idea to share it, along with the knowledge that I have gained. Now that it is possible to self-publish a paperback book on Amazon, and with my background as a graphic designer, I decided to try my hand at this book.

With such a specialised subject, it is unlikely that a traditional book publisher would risk the cost of a large print run, so Amazon's print to order system was the ideal solution for me.

I hope that you enjoy the book, much of which was written by others. My own contribution was just a few original pages, together with my research. I managed to source two rather rare, printed diaries, written by travellers on the *Remuera* some 100 years ago. It also seemed a good idea to find contemporary newspaper reports, and thanks to the generosity of Stuff Limited and the National Library of New Zealand, I have been given permission to use many newspaper stories that are now out of copyright. You can search through hundreds of interesting newspapers by visiting the excellent, and free, Papers Past website – https://paperspast.natlib.govt.nz

I re-typed the diary extracts and newspaper stories from the original books or scans, checked them carefully for errors, and set them out in these pages together with many of the photographs which have been reproduced from my personal collection.

It should be noted that the newspaper reports often appeared in print some time after the events that they referred to, but I have retained the original print date at the start of each extract.

I am very grateful to Garry Law for his advice and expertise, and for writing the Foreword to this publication. His website is well worth a visit – http://www.lawas.co.nz/info/remuera/index.htm – as you will find many stories and photographs from the launch of the *Remuera* right up to its sad demise in 1940.

David Ransom, West Sussex, UK, 2021

Introduction

This book tells of life on a ship in the 1920s, from the wealthy to the poor, who were travelling to make a new home for themselves in New Zealand, or taking long and expensive touring holidays, as they experienced the steamship *Remuera*, the highs and lows, from excitement to boredom. From a baby, born to the Twin family, James Arthur Pitcairn Twin, named after both the ship's Captain and Doctor, and the Island that the ship had recently visited, to the very sad accident which brought a sudden halt to the fun of a fancy dress party on board ship.

With over 100 rare photographs, large extracts from diaries written by holidaying passengers, and contemporary newspaper reports of voyages, it will be possible to imagine yourself on board the ship amongst this diverse collection of people from all walks of life. I have not edited their stories, so you may find that their language or point of view is not acceptable by today's standards, but history needs to be shown as it was, and not sanitised, so that we can learn from it, and not let ourselves slip back into the old ways when white assumed they were better than black

Painting of steam ships in Southampton, the *Remuera*'s home port, by night. Reproduced here from an old postcard, mailed in 1906

and the rich considered themselves superior to the poor. We still have a long way to go, but I think we are getting there, and the Black Lives Matter movement must surely help.

On each long voyage there were two major points of interest to break up the sometimes tediously long journey – the Panama Canal, and the short stop at Pitcairn Island, home of the descendants of the mutineers from HMAV *Bounty*. The *Remuera* had been the first New Zealand Shipping Company vessel to transit the Canal, back in 1916, and this amazing feat of engineering is well described by my two diarists in these pages, together with the many photographs taken by passengers and also the ship's barber who printed up his images with postcard backs and sold them from his hairdressing saloon on the *Remuera*'s main deck.

Pitcairn Island has always fascinated me. It is still a very difficult place to visit today, and there are many people in the UK who do not realise where it is, or even that it is a British territory with Islanders who hold British passports. There are not many Pitcairners today, something in the region of 40 to 50 people live on the Island. In the 1920s the population was higher, rising from 163 in 1920 to 190 by 1930. In the 1920s Pitcairn was extremely isolated, and the population relied greatly on the visits of the New Zealand Shipping Company's vessels to bring much needed supplies and correspondence. Today the Pitcairners have the internet, but there is no air strip, and only two places where small ships can berth. Large cruise ships still have to drop anchor out at sea.

The Pitcairners are presented in this book with widely differing opinions. I have never been to the Island myself, but I know people who have. I've met Pitcairners who have visited the UK in recent years and they have invariably been nice, friendly people. I find some of the opinions of them that were printed in 1920s newspapers to be offensive, but again, I have not sanitised the original text in any way. Today, life on Pitcairn is hard. If you were to suffer a serious injury or illness, you would face a difficult evacuation by sea. One Islander died in recent years because he could not reach help in time. There are fairly regular supply ships, but there is only one shop, one small school, one teacher and a doctor or nurse from New Zealand. An Islander has been trained in dentistry, but it is not his full time job. The Islanders still rely on sales of fruit and curios to passengers on visiting cruise ships to supplement their income.

David Ransom

Timeline of the 1920s

1920

Prohibition began in the United States

Southampton became the *Remuera*'s
new British home port

Voyage on 13th March to Auckland

Remuera called at Pitcairn 20th April

Voyage on 30th September to Wellington

Remuera called at Pitcairn 5th November

PROHIBITION

SPEAKEASY

SS REMUERA

1921

'Chanel No. 5' perfume created by Coco Chanel

Voyage on 5th March from Southampton

Remuera called at Pitcairn 10th April

Voyage on 25th May from Wellington –
see page 21

Voyage on 18th August from Southampton

Remuera called at Pitcairn 20th September

CHANEL
NO 5

GABRIELLE 'COCO' CHANEL

1922

The tomb of Tutankhamun discovered

Voyage on 20th February from Southampton

Remuera called at Pitcairn 7th March

Voyage on 20th July from Southampton
(not completed). Collision with SS *Marengo*
near Weymouth (21st July) – **see page 35**

Remuera's boilers converted to oil fuel
and repairs carried out

First voyage following repairs and conversion
on 14th December from Southampton

CURSE OF THE PHARAOHS

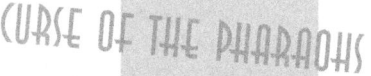

HOWARD CARTER EXAMINING THE
INNERMOST COFFIN OF TUTANKHAMUN

1923

'The Radio Times' listing magazine was first published in the UK

Remuera called at Pitcairn 13th January

Voyage on 10th May from Southampton

Remuera called at Pitcairn 5th June – **see pages 43, 49 and 51**

Voyage on 20th September from Southampton – **see page 61**

Remuera called at Pitcairn 16th October – **see page 89**

Remuera called at Pitcairn 5th December

FIRST EDITION OF THE RADIO TIMES

ON THE AIR

1924

The world's first radio play broadcast by the BBC

'The Sunday Express' became the first newspaper to publish a crossword

Voyage on 17th January from Southampton

Remuera called at Pitcairn 12th February

Remuera called at Pitcairn 30th March – **see page 123 and 143***

Voyage on 22nd May from Southampton

Remuera called at Pitcairn 17th June

Voyage in July 1924 from Wellington carrying the All Blacks on their second tour of the British Isles – **see pages 139, 141 and 146**

Remuera called at Pitcairn 6th August

Remuera called at Pitcairn 22nd October

Remuera called at Pitcairn 11th December

*30th March 1924 was a Sunday, so it appears that this article was published a year after the call at Pitcairn referred to in the newspaper.

EARLY 1920S RADIO AND HORN SPEAKER

INVINCIBLES

'THE INVINCIBLES' ALL BLACKS THAT TOURED TO THE BRITISH ISLES AND FRANCE IN 1924-25

PITCAIRN ISLAND FROM THE SEA

1925

'The Pleasure Garden' was the first film directed by Alfred Hitchcock

Voyage on 29th January from Southampton

Remuera called at Pitcairn 25th February – **see page 142**

Remuera called at Pitcairn 16th April

Voyage on 5th June from Southampton

Remuera called at Pitcairn 3rd July

Remuera called at Pitcairn 24th August

Voyage on 23rd October from Southampton

Remuera called at Pitcairn 20th November

THE PLEASURE GARDEN'
DIRECTED BY ALFRED HITCHCOCK

1926

John Logie Baird gave the first public demonstration of television

Remuera called at Pitcairn 16th January

Voyage on 12th March from Southampton

Remuera called at Pitcairn 1st June

Voyage on 30th July from Southampton

Remuera called at Pitcairn 25th August

Remuera called at Pitcairn 17th October

Voyage on 4th December from Southampton

Remuera called at Pitcairn 31st December – **see page 149**

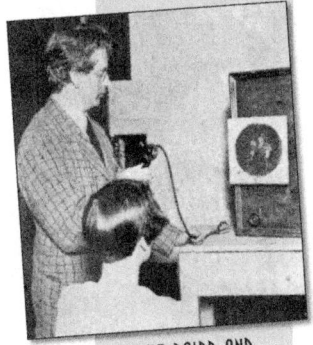

JOHN LOGIE BAIRD AND
TELEVISION RECEIVER

ON THE PANAMA CANAL

1927

Remuera wins an impromptu 11,000 mile race to New Zealand against the *Corinthic* – **see page 149**

The first transatlantic telephone call from New York City to London

Remuera called at Pitcairn 24th February

Voyage on 6th May from Southampton

Remuera called at Pitcairn 2nd June

Voyage on 30th September from Southampton

Remuera called at Pitcairn 27th October

Remuera called at Pitcairn 20th December

A WESTERN ELECTRIC CANDLESTICK PHONE FROM THE 1920S

1928

'The Jazz Singer' first 'talkie' film shown in UK

Sliced bread, and also bubble gum invented

Remuera called at Pitcairn 15th March

Remuera called at Pitcairn 6th May

Voyage on 18th July from Southampton

Remuera called at Pitcairn 2nd August

Remuera called at Pitcairn 22nd September

Voyage on 23rd November from Southampton

Remuera called at Pitcairn 22nd December

THE JAZZ SINGER' FIRST TALKIE SHOWN IN BRITAIN

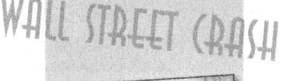

1929

Wall Street Crash sparks the Great Depression

The car radio invented

Remuera called at Pitcairn 14th February

Voyage on 12th April from Southampton

Remuera called at Pitcairn 9th May

Remuera called at Pitcairn 30th June

Voyage on 30th August from Southampton

Remuera called at Pitcairn 27th September

A CROWD GATHERS OUTSIDE THE STOCK EXCHANGE AFTER THE CRASH

New Zealand
Shipping
Company
stoker with
coal blackened
face

1920s

STEAMING BY COAL OR OIL?

Setting the record straight

Unfortunately, I need to begin this journey through the 1920s by being rather controversial. On researching the voyages of the *Remuera*, I have found that the ship continued to be powered by coal until late in 1922 when she was converted to run by oil-fired steam. The problem is that many of my source books, magazines and websites mistakenly say that the *Remuera* was converted in 1920.

The advantages of oil over coal

The change from coal-fired to oil-fired steamships was quite dramatic. Coaling a ship was a dirty and tedious job, whereas oil was simply pumped directly into the storage tanks. The boiler room of an oil-fired steamer could be as much as 25° cooler, on the Fahrenheit scale, than if coal were burned under the same boilers. Much of the additional heat in the boiler room, when using coal, was caused by opening the furnace doors to load more coal, and then much heat was lost, making coal-fired ships much less energy efficient. Labour saving was also tremendous, with the required fire-room workforce on some ships reduced by an incredible 90 per cent.*

A further advantage is energy density. Oil has a lot greater energy per ton, meaning that less tonnage of oil is required when compared to coal for the same distance of travel. This might mean more tonnage available for cargo on a cargo or mixed ship. Or, if the same tonnage is loaded, it would give more range and potentially more choice about where to stop for bunkering next.

---

*https://tinyurl.com/Oil-v-Coal

Contemporary reports confirm conversion was in 1922

As you can read in the following pages, one passenger wrote, in the published diary of his voyage, that on 25th June, 1921, "the passengers suffered great discomfort from the old method of loading coal".

The description of the 14th December, 1922, voyage from Southampton, in New Zealand's *Auckland Star* newspaper, begins with: "The *Remuera*, the first passenger steamer burning oil fuel to leave England for New Zealand...".

Also, there is the dated photographic evidence, illustrated below, that the *Remuera*'s rebuild did not take place before July 1922 when she collided with the SS *Marengo*.

This photograph, possibly taken by the ship's hairdresser Henry Keyse, shows the *Remuera* after her collision with the SS *Marengo* in July 1922. This shows the *Remuera* in her original form, prior to the refit. At this time she had five lifeboats in a row on the boat deck. After the refit, there were four in a row, perhaps larger lifeboats

It was the ideal opportunity to work on the engine room when the *Remuera* was being repaired following her collision with the SS *Marengo* in July 1922. There was a period of well over four months for this conversion to be carried out before the *Remuera* went back into service.

The following list of publications and websites have been of great help with my research.

Reference materials

Books

Pitcairn Island as a Port of Call – A Record, 1790-2010,
by Herbert Ford (McFarland & Company, Inc.), second edition, published in 2012.

Passenger Ships of Australia and New Zealand, Vol 1 1876-1912,
by P. Plowman (Doubleday, Sydney), published in 1981.

Merchant Fleets, New Zealand Shipping & Federal S.N. Co.
by Duncan Haws (TCL Publications, Hereford), published in 1985.

Crossed Flags, the histories of the New Zealand Shipping Company, Federal Steam Navigation Company and their subsidiaries by W.A Laxon, I. J. Farquhar, N. J. Kirby and F. W. Perry (World Ship Society, Gravesend), published in 1997.

Magazines

The February 1971 edition of *Sea Breezes, the magazine of ships and the sea,* includes an article by J. H. Isherwood entitled *New Zealand Liner 'Remuera' of 1911.*

Websites

Garry Law's excellent *Remuera* history website:
http://www.lawas.co.nz/info/remuera/index.htm

The P&O Heritage website, on which there is a 'Ship Fact Sheet' for the *Remuera*:
https://www.poheritage.com

New Zealand Shipping Company records for genealogy – my own website which includes passenger lists and other items from my collection which may be useful for family history research:
https://nzsc.wordpress.com

Louise Brooks, American film actress and dancer, c.1926:
The most memorable fashion trend of the 'Roaring Twenties'
was undoubtedly 'the flapper' look (Photo: Wikipedia)

1921

TRAVELS ABROAD

INTRODUCTION

The book *Travels Abroad* was published anonymously by a New Zealander who describes himself simply as 'An Aucklander'. It is an interesting little hardback book, slightly larger than A5, published in 1923 by Stott Brothers Limited of Mount Street, Halifax, West Yorkshire, UK.

The *Remuera* did not call at Pitcairn on this voyage. It was more common for calls at the Island to be made on the voyage from the United Kingdom towards New Zealand, than in the other direction. But there is an interesting account of the journey through the Panama Canal and also details of the "old method" of loading coal.

Captain J J Cameron

1921

TRAVELS ABROAD
BY AN AUCKLANDER

After a breakdown in health through overwork in Municipal and other Local Body work, my wife induced me to consider the advisability of a complete change, and we decided to visit the British Isles and part of the Continent, taking the longest route through the Panama Canal by the New Zealand Shipping Co's S.S. *Remuera*, commanded by Captain Cameron, who proved a most efficient and agreeable officer, studying the comfort of the passengers in every way.

Leaving Auckland on Sunday evening, the 22nd May, 1921, with the farewell and good wishes of our family and many friends, we had a pleasant train journey to Wellington, where we arrived at 1.10 p.m. next day.

At 3.30 p.m. on the 25th May (Wednesday), we left the Wharf at Wellington under pleasant weather conditions, and after partaking of a good dinner, we retired to rest early. Next morning we were surprised to find that it was still Wednesday, the 25th May, as we had crossed the

180° Meridian during the night and it was necessary to add one day to the calendar so as to adjust the time.

The weather conditions on this second Wednesday were unsettled and unpleasant, Father Neptune evidently objecting to any interference with the calendar without first obtaining his consent. The ladies were most considerate under the adverse conditions and indulged in the comfort of their state rooms, allowing the gentlemen to have the full benefit of the decks.

In a few days the weather improved wonderfully, and the usual committees were appointed to carry out concerts and sports, all of which were successful and reflected credit on the committee.

Mr. Skerrit, K.C., from Wellington, was one of our most prominent passengers and through his pleasant and genial ways, soon found his way to the hearts of all the passengers. His dry humour and clever little stories were much appreciated and this popularity remained during the whole voyage.

The weather gradually improved and the passengers employed their time in playing deck quoits and golf.

Passengers enjoying deck games during a 1915 voyage of the *Remuera*

On Thursday, the 9th June, we entered the latitude where flying fish were very numerous and many of the passengers were highly amused with their antics. On the following Monday, the 13th June, we saw large shoals of whales spouting all round the steamer, and on Tuesday the 14th we crossed the Equator during cool weather for this particular locality. The following day we passed Malpelo Island and on Thursday, the 16th June, we arrived at Balboa Panama too late in the day to proceed through the Canal.

It was a pleasant sensation to tread terra firma again after such a long interval on board ship, and we immediately hailed a taxi, and after exchanging our New Zealand money for American dollars, we motored out to the old historic town of Panama, formerly occupied by the Spaniards and attacked by the Pirates in such a vigorous manner that nearly all the Spanish soldiers with the exception of about seventy were killed and nearly all the buildings demolished and are now in ruins. The foliage, palms, sugar cane, pineapples and other tropical vegetation grew most luxuriantly, and some of the finest bananas which were delicious to the taste. The ruins of the old monastery still remain and the walls are covered with creepers, giving the building rather an artistic appearance with its old tower.

Balboa is a clean town beautifully laid out and planted with every variety of palm and the buildings are of modern architecture. The sanitary arrangements have been improved to such an extent that it is now one of the healthiest towns in the tropics. The very fine hospital is nicely situated on a plateau in an elevated part of the town and the grounds surrounding it have been planted with lovely palms and other tropical plants.

On Friday morning, at 6 a.m. on the 17th June, we left Balboa and entered the world-famed Canal, which is such a colossal undertaking and a tribute to engineering skill costing the American Government about eighty-five million pounds to complete. The length from shore to shore line is forty miles,

On the Panama Canal
c.1916

but from deep water in the Pacific to deep water in the Atlantic is fifty miles.

There are six locks in all, the first two from the Pacific side being Miraflores where the steamer is raised about fifty-five feet; another one and a half miles brought us to the Pedro Miguel lock where we were raised another thirty feet, making a total of eighty-five feet above sea level. We next entered the famous Culebra Cut which has been one of the greatest engineering feats yet accomplished and caused the greatest anxiety in the minds of those who carried out the work. It is three hundred feet wide at the bottom and nine miles in length necessitating the excavation of over ninety million yards of rock and earth in its construction or nearly half the amount required for the total excavation of the Canal. At Gamboa we entered the large artificial lake with its numerous tropical islands and steamed full speed ahead for about twenty-four miles, the lake covering an area of about one hundred and sixty-four square miles. We next approached the famous Gatun Dam which impounds the waters from the Chagres River and its tributaries. The walls of the dam are constructed of concrete, nearly one and a half miles long,

Two steamers passing in
Culebra Cut c.1916

nearly half a mile wide at the base, and four hundred feet
wide at the water surface. It unites the hills on either side,
thus retaining the waters of the river as in a basin and
replacing a beautiful lake where formerly there were large
areas of unhealthy swamps which were breeding grounds for
mosquitoes and disease.

The Americans are indebted to a British officer named
Colonel Ross who, after many years of scientific research in
South Africa, proved to the satisfaction of the medical world
that Yellow Jack was spread by a special kind of mosquito,
and after extensive experiments it was found that the spraying
or petroleum on the water not only killed the fly but also
exterminated the eggs. Had it not been for this wonderful
scientific discovery it is probable that the Panama Canal
would never have been completed.

The Spillway, which is located about midway in the Gatun
Dam, is built into a natural hill which stands about one
hundred and ten feet above sea level. The Spillway is capable
of discharging one hundred and fifty-four thousand cubic feet
of water per second, and on the east side is located a large

hydro-electric plant which provides electricity for operating all the machinery required to work the canal, also to run the Panama Railroad and light up the whole Canal Zone.

The length of a lock chamber is about one thousand feet, the width about one hundred and ten feet, and the depth of water over the sills about forty-one feet. The lock gates are massive steel structures seven feet thick, sixty-five feet long, and from forty-two to eighty-two feet high, weighing from three hundred to seven hundred and thirty tons each, and it is astounding with what ease they are opened, the mere pressing of a button and the marvellous power of electricity does the rest. The ships are not allowed to use their own steam

ASCENDING GATUN LOCKS. PANAMA CANAL. H.G.K.

One of the three electric mules that were used to tow steam ships, such as the *Remuera*, through Gatun Locks on the Panama Canal. This photograph was taken by Henry George Keyse. Henry worked as a barber on board the *Remuera* and took many photographs which he sold to passengers as real photo postcards. Prior to the opening of the Canal, the *Remuera*'s route took her around Cape Horn and past icebergs in the South Pacific which Henry had also photographed for postcards.

through the locks, but are drawn along by three electric mules or engines on each side, with wire hawsers connected with the steamer and attached to a cafretain on the engine so constructed that it automatically tightens or slackens as the strain of the hawser becomes too great or too slack.

We next entered the Gatun Locks, three in number, and were lowered eighty-five feet to the level of the Atlantic and then called at Colon where we took on coal in a clean, modern style, with no inconvenience to passengers, who were deeply interested in the operation.

ELECTRIC COALING STATION COLON. PANAMA   COPYRIGHT A 381q

This postcard, published c.1914 by David Aldersley, a New Zealand based photographer, shows the modern coaling station at Colon

We left Colon about 4.30 in the afternoon on Friday, the 17th June, and after passing through the opening of the extensive breakwater, we entered the Caribbean Sea which was formerly a terror to all sea-going people on account of the fearful piratical outrages committed in the olden days.

We passed Jamaica during the night of the 19th, but did not call as there was an epidemic prevalent.

On June 20th we sailed for some distance along the Cuban coast and saw a lighthouse, also an old wreck which appeared to be in a good state of preservation, afterwards passing between the Islands of Cuba and Haiti and about 8.30 the same evening with a clear atmosphere we saw Acklins Island, passing Crooked Island at midnight. After passing Santiago we saw San Salvador on Walling Island, being the windfall made by Columbus on his first voyage of discovery to the West in 1492.

On Wednesday, 22nd June, we passed The Bahamas and Nassau Islands, and after passing Old Fort Comfort, we steamed up James River and after passing a large fleet of American battle ships, we reached Newport-News and dropped anchor about eight o'clock on the evening of the 23rd June.

Early next morning we went ashore, hired a taxi and accompanied by Miss Isaacs from Auckland, we went out to Yorktown where the American Independence was finally settled and where a most high and ornate monument is erected setting forth the following: "At York in 1781, after nineteen days' siege by 5,500 Americans, 7,000 French troops, 3,500 Virginia Militia, or a total of 16,000, Earl Cornwallis, Commander of the British troops surrendered his Army consisting of 7,551 Officers and Men, 840 Seamen, 244 Cannon and 24 Standards to General Washington."

We had lunch afterwards at Ye Old York Hotel, two hundred years old, and the minced meat served to us must have been some that had been left over at the official opening of the hotel, and to improve matters, one of the negro waitresses dropped some on the floor and, after picking it up with her fingers, most solemnly handed it to a customer. We next motored to Fort Comfort which has several military barracks and hospitals, and then returned to the ship.

On account of a coal strike amongst the miners in Britain, we were delayed in taking on extra coal and did not leave Newport-News until 4.30 on the evening of Saturday, the 25th June, the passengers suffering great discomfort from the old method of loading coal.

Loading coal manually, c.1914. I'm sure that these shoeless labourers would have something to say about the writer's comment that passengers suffered "great discomfort from the old method of loading coal"

New Zealand Shipping Co.

R.M.S. "REMUERA."

VISIT THE BARBER'S SHOP
On the MAIN DECK,
PORT SIDE, AMIDSHIPS.

Hairdressing Saloon
FOR LADIES AND GENTLEMEN

Almost any article required for the voyage can be obtained there.

TOILET REQUISITES, PATENT MEDICINES, TROPICAL CLOTHING, DECK SHOES, SHIRTS, COLLARS, CAPS, VESTS, DRESS MATERIALS & HOSIERY.

Photographic Goods. Postcards and Photographs of S.S. "Remuera." Ports en Route, Panama Canal, etc.

LARGE VARIETY OF ARTICLES EXPRESSLY SELECTED SUITABLE FOR SPORTS PRIZES. MATERIALS FOR FANCY DRESS, ETC.

CADBURY'S SELECTED CHOCOLATES.

H. G. KEYSE, Hairdresser

Trade card produced by the *Remuera*'s hairdresser/
photographer to advertise items for sale in his barber
shop. Sports prizes and fancy dress items were popular

On the evening of Friday, July 1st, although the sea was rough, the passengers indulged in a fancy dress ball which proved both enjoyable and humorous.

About four days before reaching England we were delighted to receive a wireless message stating that the miners' strike was at last settled and trains would be running in a few days.

Early in the morning of Thursday, July 7th, our hearts were glad because we could see the Needles and we were not long before we were sailing up the Solent with the Isle of Wight on our right and close to Cowes Bay. The season had been so dry that the grass on the slopes of the island was quite brown and reminded us of Mount Eden and Mount Albert in a dry summer.

This small brass ship's bell was sold to passengers
on the *Remuera*, probably from the barber's shop

Although we reached Southampton early in the day and
received letters and telegrams from our English friends, it
was some time before we passed the Customs and we did not
get away until three o'clock in the afternoon. We were met at
Waterloo Station by a cousin of Mrs. Clay's and he took us
home to Finsbury Park in a motor.

*The book continued with descriptions of the author's
touring holiday throughout the UK, Europe and Canada.*

1921

VISIT TO PITCAIRN ISLAND
1ST OCTOBER

The Auckland Star.

This newspaper article is reproduced from the *Auckland Star*, New Zealand, with the kind permission of Stuff Limited (https://www.stuff.co.nz), and the National Library of New Zealand (*Papers Past* – https://paperspast.natlib.govt.nz).

Remuera's Passengers Ashore.

A Happy Community

The 'simple lifers' on lonely Pitcairn Island always look forward to the passing of the N.Z. Shipping Company's fine liner *Remuera*. Captain J. J. Cameron is a great favourite with the islanders, and they call him 'Father.' On the run across from Balboa to Auckland the ship made a brief stay to land some stores, and several of the passengers, including Sir Thomas Mackenzie, took advantage of the chance of going ashore. It is not often that passengers do get ashore, the communication between ships and the land being confined to bartering with the natives who put off in the boats. There was a bit of a sea running, but the passengers who ventured spent an interesting time, and quite enjoyed seeing the homes of the descendants of the *Bounty*. The natives are described as being very healthy, the

A large group of Pitcairn Island men and children, photographed at the boatsheds on Pitcairn Island by Henry Keyse, the *Remuera*'s hairdresser

only drawback to more than usual good looks among some of the young women being their teeth, which are not good. The people were most pleased to see the visitors, and loaded them with fruit and flowers. Some of the houses are built on European lines, and others follow the Island style of architecture. The only domesticated animals seen were goats and fowls. The natives seemed very happy, and made the most of the rare incident of having visitors ashore.

Sir Thomas Mackenzie was a Scottish-born New Zealand politician and notable explorer. He was briefly the 18th Prime Minister of New Zealand from May 1912 until July of that year, when he lost a vote of no confidence. After this he was appointed High Commissioner in London where he served until 1920.

Pitcairn Islanders alongside
the *Remuera* in 1916

1922

REMUERA REPAIRED

INTRODUCTION

The following story backs up my research which found that the *Remuera* was converted to oil in the Autumn of 1922, and not before March 1921 as reported in other publications. The writer here stated that the *Remuera* was the first passenger steamer burning oil fuel to leave England.

However, he was mistaken about the character of Bligh, who was not a "bully", although he did have a temper. History shows that William Bligh was in fact a far more lenient leader of men than many others of his time. He punished less, and did much to improve the lot of the sailors under him, all of whom were volunteers on the *Bounty*.

A different newspaper report of this particular voyage states that the *Remuera* stopped for four hours at Pitcairn Island and that a few passengers went ashore after paying the islanders 10s per head (50p). The passengers who remained on the *Remuera* watched the islanders come out in their boats, and purchased fruits and other delicacies from the boatmen.

It seems that the fare to go ashore on Pitcairn, when converted one hundred years later, taking inflation into account, equates to approximately £28.

Three photographs, possibly taken by the ship's hairdresser Henry Keyse, showing the *Remuera* after her collision with the SS *Marengo* in the English Channel in July 1922

H.M.S. "BARHAM" DIVING PARTY PLACING COLLISION MATS UNDER "REMUERA"

The *Remuera*'s first voyage following repairs and
conversion to oil fuel left Southampton on 14th December, 1922

1923

REMUERA ARRIVES

29TH JANUARY

The Auckland Star.

This newspaper article is reproduced from the *Auckland Star*, New Zealand, with the kind permission of Stuff Limited (https://www.stuff.co.nz), and the National Library of New Zealand (*Papers Past* – https://paperspast.natlib.govt.nz).

515 Passengers.

Assisted Immigrants 256

The *Remuera*, the first passenger steamer burning oil fuel to leave England for New Zealand, arrived in Auckland Harbour on Saturday, and berthed at the foot of Queen's Wharf shortly after four o'clock. She is under the command of Captain J. J. Cameron, R.N.R. Her other officers are: Chief officer, J. C. Pretty, D.S.C.; third officer H. S. Williams; fourth officer, C. D. Watt; surgeon, Dr. C. P. Ball; chief engineer, W. R. Sneddon; steward in charge, P. S. Bowen.

The *Remuera* brought 515 passengers, of whom 256 are assisted immigrants. Included in the list were Miss Lucy Jellicoe, daughter of the Governor-General, who was met by Lady Jellicoe, and Sir James Mills, managing-director of the

Union Steamship Company. Hundreds of people had secured passes on to the wharf to meet the new arrivals, and many hundreds more waited outside the gates to witness the landing of returning New Zealanders, and new New Zealanders. Mr. V. A. Mills, chief clerk of the Department of Immigration, came up specially from Wellington to see them ashore. He says that they strike him as being a very fine type of immigrant.

For Auckland there are the following nominated passengers: Males 30, women 26 and children 27. Others go to Wellington, Gisborne, Napier, Whanganui, Lyttelton and Dunedin.

Coming via Panama, the *Remuera* had a stormy week after leaving Southampton, which prostrated most of the passengers. It was the wildest Atlantic weather, following a period of exceptional peace on that occasion. The rest of the trip was thoroughly enjoyable, and especially interesting was the call at Pitcairn Island, first settled by the men famous in the historical mutiny of the *Bounty* – the men who set the bully Bligh ashore off Tofua and, under the command of Fletcher Christian, sailed for Tahiti. Here nine of the crew each secured a native wife, took with them six native Tahitians who possessed three wives between them, and finally landed on Pitcairn, where they settled and burned the brig. Pitcairn is always a source of interest to passing passengers.

Many of the *Remuera*'s passengers find it hard to forget even now of their terrifying experience after leaving Southampton. "No wonder," said one of the ship's officers. "For weeks before the *Remuera* sailed, ships arriving Home talked about the wonderful weather of the Atlantic – weather of such constant calm had never been experienced before. 'This is too good to last,' I said to myself, hoping it wasn't. Well, within a few hours after leaving Southampton we ran into a westerly gale that soon put all but the sea-hardened below. On the 21st and 22nd it blew with uncommon violence and raised tremendous seas. Standing on the bridge, it seemed as if the ship could never surmount the huge seas in front – as if it was impossible for her to lift her head in time to clear them. I have been many years at sea. I remember no seas of greater volume. Through the storm the *Remuera* showed her magnificent sea-going qualities to the full. During one 24 hours we made only 25 miles. However we averaged 11 knots to Panama and from there we came easily at 14 knots."

Commander Cameron informed the *Star* representative that the immigrants on the whole were a sterling lot of people, who came out here both willing and able to work.

"This," said Captain Cameron, "is New Zealand's golden opportunity. While unemployment is so rife at Home, you are getting a great number of the picked men of the skilled trades."

Shipping a heavy sea on a New Zealand liner.
I believe that this photograph was taken
by Peter Zerface, a barber working on the
New Zealand Shipping Company's *Ruahine*

1923

INTRODUCTION

The New Zealand Division of the Royal Navy, also known as the New Zealand Station, was formed in 1921 and remained in existence until 1941. It was the precursor to the Royal New Zealand Navy. Originally, the Royal Navy was solely responsible for the naval security of New Zealand. The passing of the Naval Defence Act 1913 created the New Zealand Naval Forces as a separate division within the Royal Navy. (Wikipedia)

1923

N.Z. NAVAL STATION
11TH JUNE

The Evening Post.

New Appointments
Some of the Officers call at Pitcairn

(From our own correspondent)
London, 4th May

By the *Remuera*, the naval officers and ratings selected for service on the New Zealand Station will leave England on 10th May. They will, doubtless, appreciate the opportunity of seeing something of Pitcairn Island, for the vessel will call there to deliver an eagerly-awaited supply of corrugated iron sheeting.

A request for this necessity, it seems, accompanied by cash, was made to Captain Cameron, on his last visit six months ago, and a pleasant surprise is in store for the islanders.

Above: Pitcairn Island photographed from the *Remuera*
Below: Islanders trading with the passengers and crew

Hearing of their need, Messrs. Lysaght, of Bristol, have forwarded nearly three times the quantity which would ordinarily be purchasable for the sum sent. Its unusual value lies in the discovery that, in an island practically devoid of natural water supply, galvanised iron roofing gives a better yield of rain water to the storage tanks than any other available substance. In addition to mails, the *Remuera* is taking out to the islanders gifts of clothing and other much-needed requirements.

All the naval officers are keen for their service in New Zealand waters. Most of them, too, have interests beyond those of duty, being well-versed in games and sport.

This article continues with a long list of appointments including, to H.M.S. *Chatham*, Lieut. Commander Penrose L. Barcroft, whose photographs appear here.

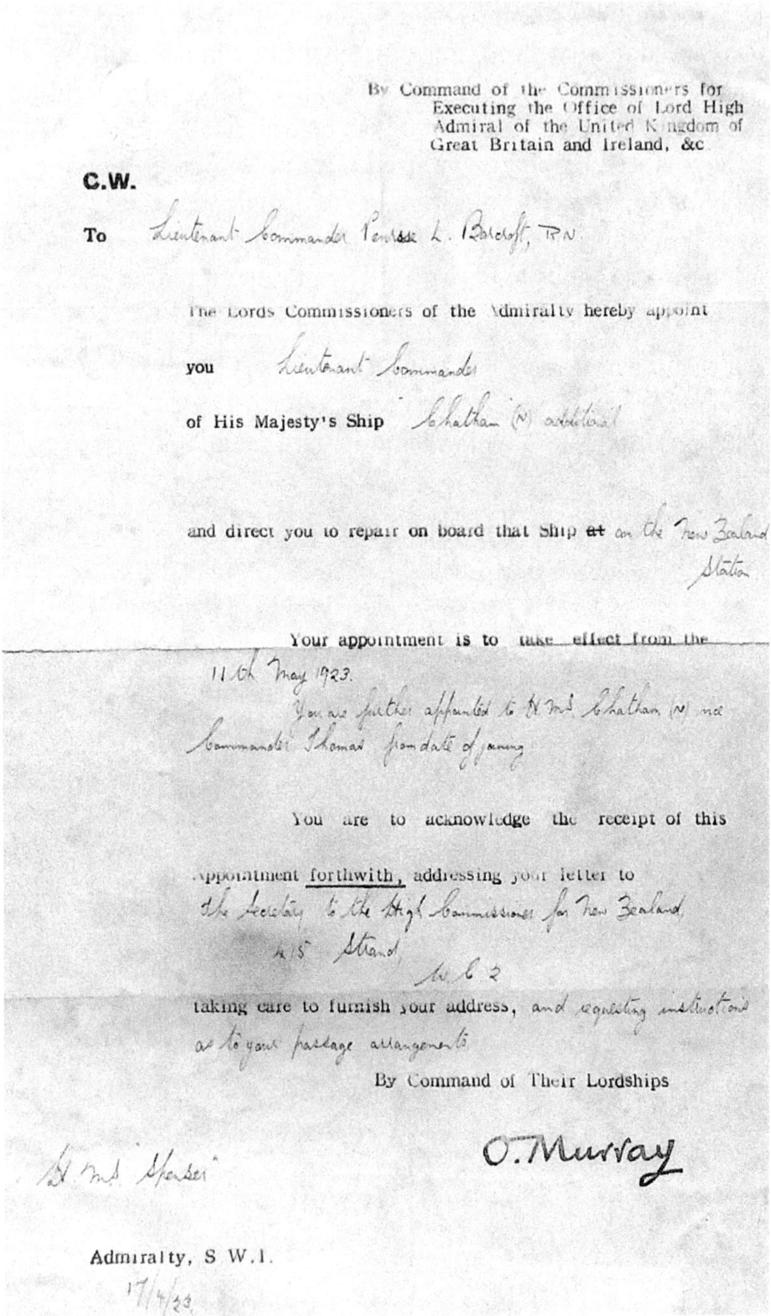

By Command of the Commissioners for
Executing the Office of Lord High
Admiral of the United Kingdom of
Great Britain and Ireland, &c

C.W.

To _Lieutenant Commander Penrose L. Barcroft, RN._

The Lords Commissioners of the Admiralty hereby appoint

you _Lieutenant Commander_

of His Majesty's Ship _Chatham (N) additional_

and direct you to repair on board that Ship at _on the New Zealand Station_

Your appointment is to take effect from the

11th May 1923.
You are further appointed to H.M.S. Chatham (N) vice Commander Thomas from date of joining

You are to acknowledge the receipt of this

Appointment **forthwith**, addressing your letter to _the Secretary to the High Commissioner for New Zealand, 415 Strand W.C.2_

taking care to furnish your address, _and requesting instructions as to your passage arrangements_

By Command of Their Lordships

O. Murray

HMS Spenser

Admiralty, S W.I.

_17/4/23_

Lieut. Commander Barcroft's letter from the Lords Commissioners of the
Admiralty appointing him to the New Zealand Station in 1923

Lieut. Commander Barcroft's caption for the above photograph, from his own album, left to right: *Mrs & Mr Miles, Christian, Sir Arthur Young, Captain Cameron*. It is likely that 'Christian' is Edgar Allen Christian who was Pitcairn's Chief Magistrate in 1923. Sir Arthur Young was a Colonial Administrator, and the 17th Governor of the Straits Settlements from 1911 to 1920. He later became the High Commissioner for the Western Pacific. Interestingly, his middle name was Henderson which is also the name of one of the islands in the Pitcairn Group, and his surname, Young, is the same as one of the *Bounty* mutineers

Pitcairn Island photographed by
Lieut. Commander Barcroft

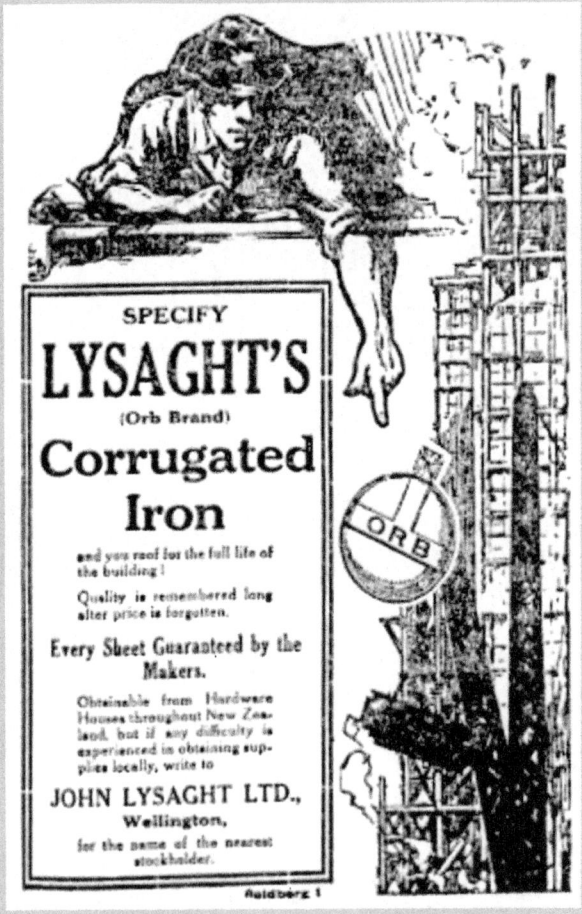

This newspaper advertisement, from 1923,
is for the Wellington, New Zealand, branch
of John Lysaght Ltd.

1923

PITCAIRN ISLAND

16TH JUNE

The Auckland Star.

This newspaper article is reproduced from the *Auckland Star*, New Zealand, with the kind permission of Stuff Limited (https://www.stuff.co.nz), and the National Library of New Zealand (*Papers Past* – https://paperspast.natlib.govt.nz).

Visit by *Remuera*

An Affecting Experience

On a former occasion of the steamer *Remuera* calling at Pitcairn Island, a sum of money was entrusted to Captain Cameron with which to purchase corrugated iron for roofing the cottages of the inhabitants, and when the *Remuera* arrived in England, John Lysaght, Ltd., generously undertook to supply three times the amount that could be covered by the purchase money. This was landed at Pitcairn recently on the *Remuera*'s voyage from Southampton to Auckland, the islanders being delighted with the result of their investment.

It was fine weather when the steamer hove-to about a mile off shore, and the boats which put off from the island contained a number of women and children, who rejoiced in the opportunity to explore the big ship. The visitors brought baskets of delicious fruit, flowers, and necklaces for sale and barter, and were made the recipients of many gifts of clothing from the passengers, who were greatly interested in the romantic history and the charming, childlike manners of these isolated people.

'God Be With You Till we Meet Again,' sang the Pitcairners, as, having returned to their boats, they watched regretfully the drawing away of the liner that had brought a few hours of such joy to their simple hearts.

Pitcairn Island, photographed by New Zealand Shipping Company hairdresser Henry George Keyse

1923

LONELY PITCAIRN

26TH JUNE

The Evening Post.

A world of its own. How the people are faring.
'An unspoiled naturalness.'

The public has always had a sympathetic interest in the people of Pitcairn Island, a lonely British possession in the mid-Eastern Pacific, not only on account of their unique history, but on account of the fact that they are more or less isolated from the rest of the world. Although well supplied with mails, the Pitcairn Islanders seldom receive visits from their fellow-beings, and the passengers of any vessel that does stop at the island for any length of time are assured of a very rousing welcome from the inhabitants. Such was the experience of the passengers of the *Remuera*, which, on its last trip from Home to New Zealand, called at the island and gave those on board the unique opportunity of spending some time ashore. In an interview with the representative of *The Post*, Mr. William Lowson, one of the passengers, gave an interesting account of the conditions obtaining at Pitcairn.

"Every one of the passengers on the *Remuera*," said Mr. Lowson, "must be glad that the Captain's interest in the islanders made it possible to pay them a visit, and the large majority are the richer for an experience that comparatively few are privileged to enjoy. Wonderful as is the Panama Canal, with an attraction all its own, the transparently genuine people of the island so captivated their visitors that the opinion was freely expressed on board that the few hours spent with them were the most delightful of the whole voyage. The arrival was in the middle of the night – 3 a.m. The stopping of the engines, followed by the swish and bang of a rocket, announced to ship and island that we were there. Only a portion of the land was visible from the porthole. There, in the dim moonlight, lay the place which was to us only a name.

With an eye to business

"The rocket was hardly needed. Not long after we had stopped three boats were alongside. On deck, passengers had already gathered, half-clad for the most part, eager to meet the folks of whom they had heard. Nor had they long to wait. The men came up the rope ladder, carrying full baskets of fruit and curios, as easily as the average person walks upstairs. Business has no fixed hours there – it is all a matter of opportunity, and in a little while the short supplies were sold. The ship was not expected for three days – she had made a record passage in 26 days. While two of the boats received cargo brought to order and gifts from the 'outside world,' the third hurried back to the island. It was 'all hands on deck' to gather fruit. Two of the passengers, a lady and gentleman, who had for years been corresponding with the islanders and sending parcels, were in the boat. They had chanced to book the very vessel whose commander, Captain

Cameron, is the person most conversant with the island, past and present, with an interest in the people equal to his knowledge, and consent was readily given to go ashore.

"Mr. McCoy, the natural leader, though not at present the chief magistrate, took them in charge, and conducted them to the village. There they met those to whom they were but a name. There was time to see only a portion of the place, including the church and the storehouse, where is placed the tenth of the produce, which the people set aside to God, to be sold and the proceeds sent for missionary work. The cemetery was also visited, with its neatly-kept graves, for people die there as elsewhere, though it be like a paradise, and in many ways might belong to another scheme of things than the world we live in. Accidents happen, and two of the graves had pathetic inscriptions to the memory of fine young men crushed on a stormy day – under an overturned boat.

A picturesque scene

"Everything was clean and well-kept. The houses, built of wood, had little of polish, but were comfortable, without luxury. From the main road, winding paths went off on both sides, into the bush, where the buildings stood, here and there, not in rows, with an absence of planning, which made for picturesqueness. The bell had rung, and from all quarters fruit-laden men, women, and children were hurrying to the cliff path down to the boats. On the beach was a bee-hive scene, with noise enough for a country fair.

"The cargo was landed, and the boats were filled again – crowded – with nearly the whole community, loaded with the fruit for sale. The visitors were carried to a boat, which was pushed off. Bounty Bay is small; with a nasty turn only a little way from the shore, calling for skill, strength, and steadiness, especially when there is any sea on. Past this, the mast was shipped, the sail hoisted, and in a short time the *Remuera* was reached. All swarmed on deck, the women and children negotiating the wobbly rope-ladder as easily as ascending their steep path from landing place to village. The goods were hoisted on ropes.

No profiteering

"The deck was a busy place. Buyers and sellers were making the most of the opportunity for mutual advantage, for such it was. Some passengers, after their experiences at Balboa, in the Panama Canal Zone, were a little inclined to bargain, but the majority bought without haggling, bearing in mind Captain Cameron's statement that the price asked was fair. The captain was right. 'To profiteer,' that war-born verb, is not in the vocabulary of the islanders. About 200 oranges, 80 bananas, 20 lemons, and 10 limes for 18s! That is what one company of six young men rejoiced in. Both parties were satisfied. It was an example of the advantages of direct dealing between producer and consumer. One man asked 3s 6d for a quantity, and was offered 2s 6d, which he refused. He would not reduce, and after a lot of talking on the part of the bargain-seeker, he picked up his basket and walked away. "Stop, I'll give you 3s 6d." He kept moving. "I will not sell to you now, you are not a just man." And he did not.

A real friend

"Cameras were busy. Groups were formed, and before the picture was taken, half a dozen Kodaks were in readiness to follow on. The whistle blows. Good-byes are said, and much handshaking and good wishes are passed as the men and women went over the side. There is no doubt as to the Islanders' affection for Captain Cameron. He is known as the 'Father of the Island,' the people themselves speak of him as their best friend. Trouble does not count with him, when rendering real help is concerned, and the recent improvement in their circumstances and outlook is largely due to his practical interest in their welfare. This time he brought a large quantity of galvanised iron for roofing the houses. He interested the manufacturers, Messrs. Lysaght, of Bristol, England, who generously sent three times what the money was worth. Many of the people brought flowers. To every query as to price, there was one answer, 'They are not for sale, they are for our friend, Captain Cameron.'

A touching farewell

"Two of the boats had cast off; the third waited for the late-leavers. Then came the sweetest and most striking incident of the whole visit – of the whole trip. The occupants of the two boats commenced to sing as they drifted away. It was the farewell hymn – 'In the Sweet By and By.' The sound was arresting, it gripped the long line of passengers leaning on the rail above. So unexpected, so beautiful and affecting were the words, in part song, so obviously sincere their action, small wonder that many women were in tears. 'Cast off there!' It was an officer's voice, calling to the boat below. The engines began to move, but cast off they did not. They, too, sang: 'Jesus, Lover of My Soul, Let Me to Thy Bosom Fly.' Nearer than the others their voices, blending well, were more distinctly heard, but there was no overpowering, no discord. The *Remuera* moved, still they held on. Not till the last verse was ended was the rope released, and they drifted past the stern towards their companions, to the accompaniment of waving good-byes and shouted good wishes.

"It was a perfect farewell, one of those incidents which remain in the memory, bringing a smile to the face, and a tender look to the eye whenever clearly recalled. We no longer wonder at the warm interest taken by our Captain in such a people, whose unspoiled naturalness has no counterpart anywhere in the world."

1923

PITCAIRN ISLAND LECTURE
13TH JULY

The Evening Post.

This newspaper article is reproduced from the *Evening Post*,
New Zealand, with the kind permission of Stuff Limited
(https://www.stuff.co.nz), and the National Library of New Zealand
(*Papers Past* – https://paperspast.natlib.govt.nz).

A lecture of a particularly interesting nature was
given by Captain Cameron of the steamer *Remuera*,
in St. Mark's School on Wednesday, the subject
being Pitcairn Island. The lecturer briefly traced the
history of the island from its original discovery by Carteret
in 1767 to the present day, mentioning the famous mutiny
of the *Bounty*, and Captain Bligh's perilous voyage of
nearly 4000 miles in an open boat from the Friendly Islands
to Timor. The present condition of the island, its interesting
inhabitants, and their quaint customs were described,
and added interest was given by the fact that two of the
islanders who are making the round trip in the *Remuera*
were among the audience. The lecture was illustrated
by an excellent collection of lantern slides, which
Captain Cameron has collected from many sources,

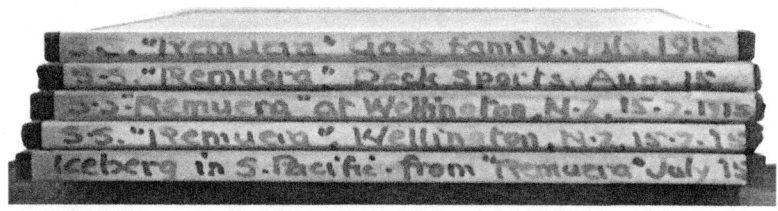

These lantern slides, from a 1915 voyage of the
Remuera, or a very similar selection, may have formed
part of Captain James Cameron's lecture in 1923

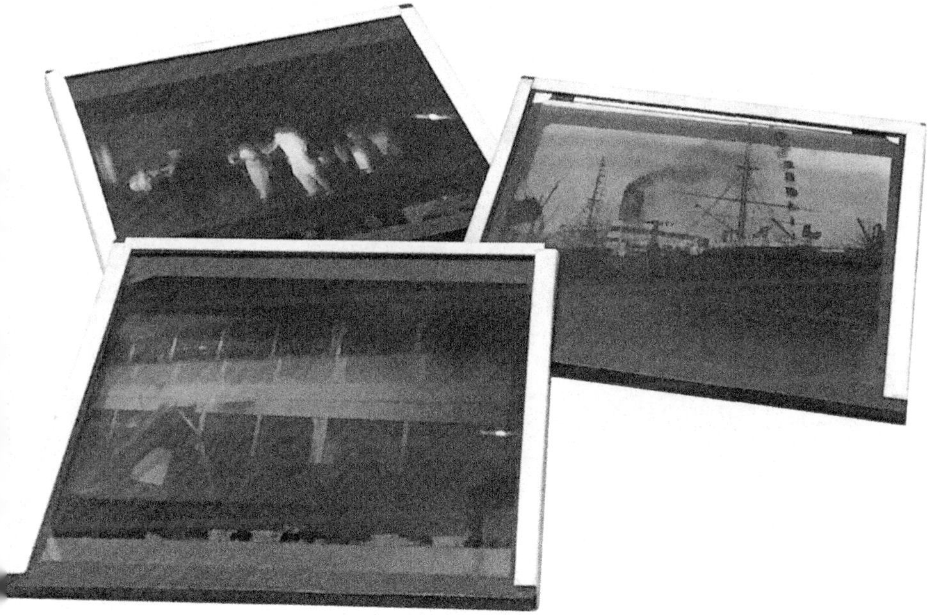

mainly for the purpose of interesting passengers by
the *Remuera* on the voyage out. A hearty vote of
thanks was accorded the lecturer on the motion
of Mr. Button.

The front cover of *Round The World 1924* which is
a very large (376mm x 308mm) self-published hardback
book. The extract which follows covers the first
section of the voyage, up to and including the
books's anonymous family's arrival in New Zealand

1923

A FASCINATING DIARY

INTRODUCTION

The following diary was written by the owner of a printing company. He had the distinct advantage of being able to have his book published as a large hardback for distribution amongst his family and friends. I do not think it was printed in large quantities because it is very difficult to obtain a copy today.

The section reproduced here includes the family's complete voyage by the *Remuera* as well as a fascinating account, written by the author's son, of his short visit to Pitcairn Island.

I feel that I must warn readers that although the racist language used in parts of this account is, of course, totally unacceptable by today's standards, I do not agree with editing history, and it should be read with some acknowledgement of 1920s attitudes to life, even though it seems very wrong today. Thankfully we have come a long way since then as a human race (although there is still, unfortunately, a long way to go), and I apologise if you are offended at times when reading this account. For this reason, and also because the author did not use any surnames in his published account, I have preserved his anonymity in my book. He simply referred to himself as 'WW'. With so many records being available online today, it is fairly easy to find a passenger list for this voyage, and to work out the full names of the people in this diary.

I imagine that the author's employees at his printing works may not have been too impressed with their employer's descriptions of his boredom at times during the voyage!

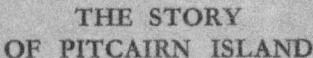

THE STORY
OF PITCAIRN ISLAND

AND

THE MUTINY
OF THE BOUNTY

BY

Captain J. J. CAMERON,
R.N.R., Rtd.

*With
the Compliments of*

THE NEW ZEALAND SHIPPING COMPANY,
LIMITED.

THE STORY OF PITCAIRN ISLAND
AND
THE MUTINY OF THE BOUNTY

In the year 1787 the British Government fitted out the armed vessel "Bounty" for the purpose of proceeding to the South Seas for young breadfruit plants to be conveyed to the West Indies where, in the opinion of Sir Joseph Banks, the eminent botanist who had visited Tahiti with Captain Cook, they could be successfully cultivated.

This voyage was undertaken in consequence of a petition to King George III by certain merchants and planters who had heard how widespread and prolific the breadfruit was in the South Sea Islands and believed it would make a cheap and suitable food for the negro slaves on their West Indian plantations.

William Bligh was appointed to the "Bounty" in the dual capacity of Captain and purser; he was at that time a Lieutenant in the Navy, 33 years of age and had been sailing-master under Captain Cook in H.M.S. "Resolution." The "Bounty" was fitted out at Deptford on the Thames under the supervision of Captain Bligh and Sir Joseph Banks, the advice of the latter as to the best method of keeping the tender young plants alive during a long sea voyage being of great value, and the vessel's hold was specially prepared for that purpose.

The breadfruit tree is about the size of a common English oak and can be seen at Panama. It has large spreading branches and the foliage is of a deep olive green. The fruit itself, which is round in shape and about the size of a melon, is pulled before it is quite ripe and roasted, then the thick outer rind having been removed, the inside is found to be somewhat like wholemeal bread. It is pleasant to the palate, a nutritious food and, as it bears during nine months of the year, is a staple article of diet amongst the natives where it grows.

Two days before Christmas, the "Bounty" sailed from St. Helens Roads for the South Seas. She was a sloop of war of 215 tons. Her dimensions were 91 feet in length over-all, 24 feet beam, and 10 feet depth of hold and her complement

1

The front cover (above) and first page (left) of a pamphlet written by Captain James Cameron, and published by the New Zealand Shipping Company

1923

ᚱOUND THE WORLD
S.S. ᚱEMUEᚱA, SOUTHAMPTON TO NEW ZEALAND VIA PITCAIRN ISLAND

Thursday, 20th September, 1923

Today the great adventure really begins. Of course, everybody was wide awake when the alarm clock went off at 3-15 a.m., the whole crowd having had a semi-sleepless night from excitement. The little 'Standard' was already loaded up and

SS *Remuera*

SHIP'S LOG.

Date.	Lat.	Long.	Dist.	Total.	Remarks.
Sept. 20	N.	W.			Leave Southampton.
,, 21	48·39	6·42	254		Strong wind, high sea.
,, 22	45·26	13·11	328	582	Fresh breeze, rough sea.
,, 23	41·51	19·05	335	917	Light airs, heavy swell.
,, 24	38·08	24·27	332	1,249	Gentle breeze, moderate sea.
,, 25	36·19	31·12	349	1,598	Light breeze, slight sea.
,, 26	34·13	37·41	340	1,938	Moderate wind, moderate sea.
,, 27	31·55	43·35	327	2,265	Fresh breeze, rough sea.
,, 28	29·08	49·29	350	2,615	Moderate wind, moderate sea.
,, 29	26·23	55·12	345	2,960	Light airs, moderate swell.
,, 30	23·13	60·26	343	3,303	Gentle breeze, slight sea.
Oct. 1	19·56	65·23	339	3,642	Light breeze, smooth sea.
,, 2	16·35	70·29	353	3,995	Light breeze, smooth sea.
,, 3	13·12	75·42	364	4,359	Strong breeze, moderate sea.
,, 4	At Colon.		341	4,700	Light breeze, smooth sea.
,, 5	Transit of Canal		43	4,743	Steamy heat and rain.
,, 6	5·0	80·05	290	5,033	Light breeze, slight sea.
,, 7	0·50	85·30	323	5,356	Light breeze, slight sea.
	S.				
,, 8	2·50	89·25	344	5,700	Light breeze, slight sea.
,, 9	5·51	94·23	345	6,045	Moderate breeze, slight sea.
,, 10	8·50	99·22	347	6,392	Gentle breeze, slight sea.
,, 11	11·50	104·28	351	6,743	Moderate breeze, moderate sea.
,, 12	14·36	109·40	345	7,088	Moderate breeze, moderate sea.
,, 13	17·08	114·42	328	7,416	Gentle breeze, moderate sea.
,, 14	19·53	120·07	350	7,766	Moderate breeze, moderate sea.
,, 15	22·30	125·42	350	8,116	Light breeze, slight swell.
,, 16	25·03	130·04	288	8,404	Pitcairn, 8 a.m.—1 p.m. Moderate sea, moderate swell.
,, 17	27·11	135·27	314	8,718	Moderate breeze, strong swell.
,, 18	29·30	141·15	336	9,054	Gentle breeze, slight sea.
,, 19	31·45	147·25	346	9,400	Moderate gale, very rough sea.
,, 20	33·25	153·24	320	9,720	Fresh breeze, rough sea.
,, 21	34·28	159·30	310	10,030	Gentle breeze, heavy swell.
,, 22	35·24	166·22	342	10,372	Light airs, smooth sea.
,, 23	36·07	173·12	336	10,703	Fresh wind, moderate sea.
,, 24	36·22	179·47	319	11,027	Strong wind, rough sea.
,, 26					

This table is reproduced from the original book,
'Round The World, 1924' by W.W.

faithfully took us all to Southampton, well up to scheduled time. Uncles and aunts and other old friends refused to let us depart without coming down to see the last of us, and we had quite a cheery send off. A rough wind was tearing round old Southampton and an ominously low barometer gave us many qualms as to future discomforts. Down along the Docks we drove, passing the great giant *Aquitania* on the way to our *Remuera*. Two hours of confusion, bustle and goodbyes and two tugs started to pull us out into the fairway.

We were away well by 2-30 and great interest was exhibited by the young tyros in travel over everything. Going was all very nice until we dropped our pilot near the Needles and most of the passengers had their last meal for some days. There seems to be a very motley collection of passengers – quite an interesting crowd for future reference. All go off to bed about 8 p.m., as considerable movement is just commencing.

Friday, 21st September

Ship's log reads at noon – Strong wind, high sea, 254 miles. This means a lot to the old travellers, and to the new ones, is the wordy evidence that life is not all beer and skittles. If asked, and they could mutter a few words with a meaning, they would willingly exchange this world for any old other one. Boreas and Co. have been, and are, in full blast from the South West. Our Bynk, Val, Sylvia and old Laura, are all wishing they were dead, and I am sure they sincerely wish that they had never started. Jon is in great form and is a good sailor. Mum is, as usual, splendid and not affected in the least, and looks after us all like the real mother she is.

Saturday, 22nd September

Everyone who was going to be sick, has been so sick that they can't be sick any more, and they look a poor, washy lot. A passenger, who is just recovering, says that last year he went via Cape Horn and no weather so bad as this was experienced. Today is nasty – windy – dull – rainy, with a rough sea. There is nothing to do and we can only doze, read and hope for better times ahead. Poor little Skibosh is very poorly and Mum is having a bad time with her. It really has been a three days and nights of nightmare. Only four women down to dinner and none in the first class. Today, places are being allotted for permanent positions at table in the saloon. The children's meal, being an hour before the grown-ups, Laura and Jon going to that with Skibosh. We others had hoped to have a table to ourselves in a corner, but the head steward informs us that Mum and I are requested to occupy the position of honour, at the right hand of Commander Cameron at centre. We feel we can hardly stand the strain of such limelight and request that we shall be all together in our corner, but no good, here we are

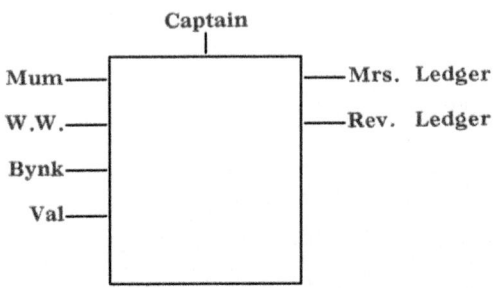

It seems that the Captain honours the second class twice a week, by presiding at a meal and if he is not there, one or another of the Chief Officers takes his place.

Sunday, 23rd September

All last night there was a heavy swell running and quite a lot of people had bad nights. Now today there is no wind, or very little, and a glorious blue sky and sea, but still the big swell which rolls us about quite a lot. 'Molly's' and 'dolphins' have shown up and added to the general interest.

Have come across the Chief Engineer, who is quite talkative for a Scotsman. Have learnt that we are to call at Pitcairn Island, which seems intensely interesting. More of that in due course. The passengers seem to be most anxious to help one in any way possible on the other side. All our invalids have recovered except Ski, who is a little better and sleeping in a sunny corner of the deck. By tea-time the gorgeous sunshine and blue has all fugged up and my little Aneroid has started off 'down.' White horses are now showing up again, and Boreas and Co. seem to be preparing to have another go at us. Mum was anxious about Ski, so went and had a consult with the doctor, who turned out to be the man I thought was Chief Engineer. Quite a nice man, in whom one could have confidence. She is gradually getting better I think, if only this cursed wind business would shut up. Anyway, it's only a few more days, thanks be! before we are out of the roaring forties.

I must not forget to mention that today, the Great Presence appeared and presided at midday meal. A truly awe-inspiring personage, with tremendous gravity of presence. 'Our Admiral' isn't in it. Mum did nobly and was well assisted by the Bynk during the ordeal. It appeared again at dinner, which was just as 'heavy.'

Monday, 24th September

Thanks be! the threatened Valkyries went off sideways, and left us with a rising glass and sea rapidly getting calmer. Today has been gorgeous and full of interest. A fairly calm sea and a dead steady boat. About noon we sighted St. Miguel, the largest island of the Azores group, and all afternoon we passed along its S.E. shore. It was 25 miles long with a population of 117,000 people. It is a mountainous island with a highest point of 3,600 feet, most beautiful in outline, valleys, forests and cultivated land growing crops of corn, flax, etc. Many fine villages and towns were distinctly in view and several times we were near enough to see the inhabitants on the shore watching our steamer. We were from one to five miles off along the whole coast.

All the passengers seem now to have recovered from the nightmare of the recent bad weather and Committees are being formed for Sports and Music. There seems to be a great lack of talent in this direction. Mum, Bynk and I are on the Committees. The real Chief Engineer presided today, and has taken a fancy to our boys and invited them to go down into the bowels of our Leviathan to see his beloved engines. This is to be a treat for them tomorrow. A perfect sub-tropical evening with full moon ended the day. It is now getting steamy and very hot, particularly in the cabins.

Tuesday, 25th September

Another gorgeous day of blazing sunshine. Amusements committees got to work and have really achieved quite a lot. A diligent search for talent has found a small fat flapper, who can play for the dancing mob, who, I suppose, will henceforth occupy the best deck every evening with their ceaseless senseless wig wag. Competition lists and events are now posted up. These include all the really 'clever things,' such as throwing rope rings on to a peg or bags of sand on to squares marked out, or deck tennis, or threading a needle with your eyes shut and varieties innumerable.

Over the edge of the ship, today, nothing of interest has happened. Not a bird or fish has been seen; just the blue ocean ruffled by a stiff breeze, a blue like a sapphire, of an intensity that cannot be seen near land. It is really getting hot now and not even a sheet is wanted as a covering at night. The fans are on full in the cabins and we already perspire, not being acclimatised to this glorious warmth. I think, tomorrow I will try a night on deck and take the boys. Have had a few confabs with various passengers, but have not found a kindred spirit, so do not expect to see much of them.

All of us are now fit except for a bad attack of toothache to Laura, and Mum, who is not yet quite herself, after her terrible week. Taking things all round, we all now are glad, I think, to be alive and on the way. We wish, however, we could have news of Home.

Wednesday, 26th September

Last night things really got on a lot. The barrier on the promenade deck was removed, the deck piano was put into commission and 'God's chosen' came and honoured us with their presence and danced to the accompaniment of the fat flapper. Now today has also been a great stir – competitions in full blast, gorgeous weather still and a slight sea. Evening dancing again with a few songs. Our Mum performed

'Coolan Ddu,' bringing much applause, but I felt too nervous to risk the fat flapper in public. Hope to try a practice some time. It would make such a difference if there was a good pianist on board. Quite a nasty suspicious roll and a pitch or two about bed-time is making us anxious.

Thursday, 27th September

Woke up to a rattle of banging doors and hissing spray dangerously near the porthole at 5 a.m. Ship is rolling about badly again. Swish, comes in through the port a big dash of spray. So close up. Now the stuffiness of the cabins is very bad. Lots of vacant places at table today. The crowd all look and feel like bees on a cold wet summer morning – half stupefied. It is really a rough day today and rainy and quite nasty, but very warm. All the officers and stewards are arrayed in shining clean white uniforms and if only the weather would be fine, and a smooth sea, it would be just heaven. Bynk is feeling a little queer, otherwise nothing much wrong and all the others are still in great form. Mum seems born to it and goes down forward to meet the bounce and turmoil of the seas as they bang into us.

By the way, the two Pitcairn Islanders, of whom the *Daily Mail* made a fuss this last summer, are on board as part of the crew.* Found Bynk confabbing with one of them, who has invited her "to go on the Island and stay there." I shall have to keep an eye on this matter. Pitcairn Island is half way from Panama to Auckland.

The sea is going down a bit now (dinner time), 6 p.m., thanks be! and there are no white horses and tearing wind, but still a big swell running, coming on to our starboard bows, and heavy rain squalls with thunder and lightning are visible on different parts of the horizon. Occasionally one comes over the ship. Rather a boring day.

---

*There are two newspaper stories, dated 15th and 27th October 1923, about the Pitcairn Islanders' visit to London on pages 111 and 115

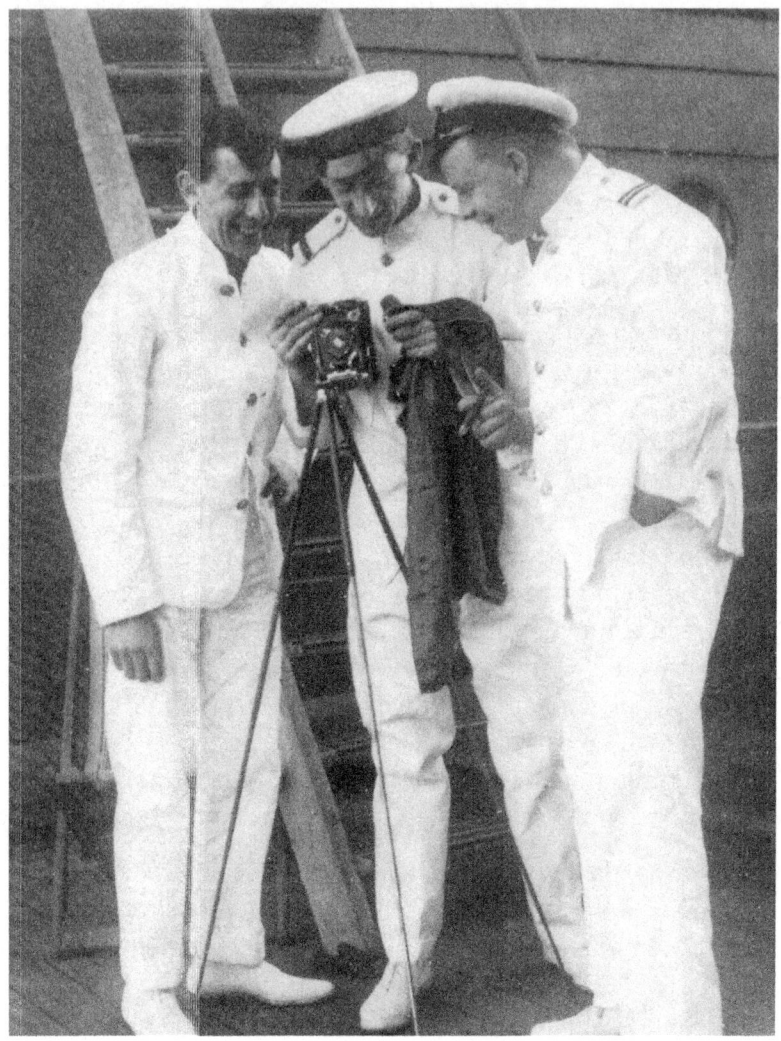

Members of the New Zealand Shipping Company crew in their whites

Friday, 28th September

Wind has changed to N.N.E., bringing a nasty tummy-turning swell along from the starboard quarter. Heat very great, burning sun on the deck all morning but cloudy after lunch. Big evening entertainment, Mum being on the programme to sing. Got through her song well and was encored. Pianists are very weak.

Saturday, 29th September

Beautiful hot day and calm sea, ending up with the most gorgeous sunset ever seen. Crowds gave up part of dinner to come out and watch it. Not a word artist living could do half justice to it. Getting hard up for news for diary. Nothing happens. Nothing to be seen but a few flying fish. Have not seen a single ship yet.

Sunday, 30th September

A great day for all this Puritan crowd. They've been at it since early morning, with services somewhere or other. Mum, Val and Bynk in the choir. I took care of Skibosh, with Laura.

A gorgeous day, we crossed the tropic of Cancer about noon today and it really is hot. A notice is out, that all who care to, may sleep on deck, so am going up with Val to try it. Poor old boy has a temperature tonight. I am afraid it is a touch of sun, as the heat has been blistering today.

The ship's officers are becoming more approachable now. Bynk is well on the way of getting off with one and Mum with another, so I shall get a rest!! I suppose.

There is The Presence (Commander) quite unapproachable. Then Snubbie, the First Officer, we haven't much use for him. Then 'Horace' the Second, which is Mum's favourite, and then Bynk has appropriated 'Blue Eyed Bertie' quite a nice boy and a dream to look at. I think he is the hero of Florodora. Then there is the Cherub, who is very nice and rather shy. I expect developments on Monday night at a big dance to be held on the full first and second mutual deck. I am afraid I shall get very bored with this voyage as there is nothing whatever of any interest to do.

Monday, 1st October

Another blazing day, stinking hot. Woke as usual in the tropics at dawn, after a lovely sleep on deck to watch a magnificent sunrise at 5-50. Baths, etc., as usual and loll about till lunch, then went down over the engine room. Quite a wonderful experience. I didn't understand anything about the huge machinery, but wouldn't have missed it. My! the heat. It was 130° and damp. The iron ladders burnt your feet and you were given rags to hold on to the rails by or they would have burnt your hands. I would like to have had John Millburn with me or another engineer pal.

The passenger crowd is about the funniest lot I have ever struck. There are also about 40 or 50 children on board from 1 to 12 years of age or so. The place is like a Zoo for noise and general turmoil. We have found a place up forrard where we all go to spend the most of our time and get out of most of it. Tonight, there is a dance on which is always a nuisance.

We can see on our port side a lighthouse, which must be the Island of Puerto Rico. We pass through a channel between Puerto Rico and Haiti. This is the entrance to the Caribbean Sea, called the Mona Passage. Mona is a small island in the middle of the channel, on which are wild cattle, goats, pigs and tortoises. Santo Domingo Haiti is the second largest island in the West Indies. Area about 30,000 square miles, about the same size as Ireland and politically is two republics. It was discovered by Columbus in 1492 and called Hispaniola or New Spain. Afterwards called Santo Domingo. Then occupied by peaceable races called Arawaks, numbering about two millions. They called the island Haiti (mountainous). In 12 years the Spaniards had disposed of nearly half of them by flogging, by burning at the stake in the name of religion, and by working them to death in the mines and fields. In 30 years from the discovery by Columbus the entire race had been swept off the face of the earth for ever. To replace them, black slaves were imported from Africa and they increased rapidly.

In 1785, the western part of the island passed under the sovereignty of France and when the French Revolution broke out, the blacks were emancipated. As soon as they were free, the liberated slaves massacred the entire French population, men, women and children. Since then Haiti has been a black independent state. The negroes have had it to themselves and have not been interfered with. Nominally they are R.C.'s, but the majority of them have reverted to the heathen abominations of their forefathers and practice Voodoo worship, child sacrifice and cannibalism. It is the country where black rules white and under that rule its towns have become the foulest and nastiest in the world, while the jungle has overrun the beautiful French plantations and estates.

The eastern portion of the Island is the black republic of Santo Domingo and is a little less degraded than Haiti. The isle is the most fertile in the West Indies, but its commerce is almost completely destroyed by perpetual revolutions and misgovernment, lawlessness and bloodshed.

Tuesday, 2nd October

Weather still perfect. Had a glorious sleep on deck last night and woke to a beautiful sunrise. Nothing to do, of course, all day, but in the evening Capt. Cameron gave a lantern lecture

Postcard view of the boat deck, SS *Remuera*

of Panama Canal History. Very interesting, although perhaps, a bit too long. A bit of a sea had got up and the noise of the sea and the wind made it difficult to concentrate. We are due tomorrow at Colon and are much looking forward to it.

Wednesday, 3rd October

I made a mistake, we shall not be in to Colon until tomorrow about noon. The heat is still overpowering and although I enjoy every minute of it, the others are reduced to a state of flab. The cabins and saloons are unbearable and we all sleep on deck. It is between 80° and 90° day and night. Now I must close up because they collect the mail tonight.

Thursday, 4th October

Woke up in a steamy swelter. The heat is really awful today. Even I will cry "Enough! Enough!" By 11 a.m. it has clouded hazily up with a glare on the water and a following breeze. Land ho!! and with the glasses we can make out South America. Very interesting for the next hour cruising along the coast and watching the great mountains and forests. The sky has fugged up, and by 12-15 a terrific thunderstorm has developed with heavy rain and blotted out all view of the shore, but it has brought along a refreshing coolness. I spent a day, three days ago, getting up a sunburn, and now I am paying much for it. My underlip has swelled up to double size and burns like a fire. It is very painful. Curse them. Just drawing into Colon. Very interesting. Doctor's launch puts out and he comes aboard to pass everybody. These formalities are soon completed and we pass into the Canal.

It is the rainy season and of course it is raining all the time. How beautiful and refreshing the tropical verdure is after a fortnight's water and sky alone. For a few miles it is very narrow with dense tropical jungle on both sides. Some interesting birds of several kinds display themselves to us.

Real photograph postcard, published by the New Zealand based
photographer David Aldersley, showing Gatun Locks

Now we are drawing up to the great Gatun Locks. There are
three, in immediate succession, lifting us up 87 feet to the
level of the Gatun Lake. To an engineer, I suppose, it would
be interesting, but we can only gape and think what a
wonderful animal man is. It is raining all the time and
photography would not be much good.

The next reach is across Gatun Lake. This Lake was made by
damming up the Gatun end of an enormous valley and letting

Real photograph postcard, possibly by New Zealand Shipping Company
hairdresser Henry Keyse, showing Gatun Lake

WATERFALL GATUN LAKE. PANAMA CANAL.   P.Z. Photo.

Real photograph postcard by New Zealand Shipping Company
hairdresser Peter Zerface. Peter spent most of his career
on the *Ruahine* and *Rangitane* ships

it fill with the water from the surrounding hills and their rivers. Now it is an enormous artificial lake, with islands dotted about covered with dense vegetation.

Soon we pass out of the lake into the canal proper again, which is wide enough to allow two ocean liners to pass quite easily. The narrow part of the Canal makes you realise what a stupendous undertaking the Panama Canal was. We learn today that our boat, the S.S. *Remuera*, was the first ocean liner to go through the Canal. This Canal is far more interesting than the Suez. It does so reek of the tropics. The foliage and intensity of the greenery densely covering all the hilltops, tells of the heavy rainfall of 145 inches, annually.

Another real photograph postcard, possibly by New Zealand Shipping Company hairdresser Henry Keyse. These postcards would have been sold to passengers from his Hairdressing Saloon on the *Remuera*

We have now crossed all the high level and have to descend two locks here at Pedro Miguel and then cross Miraflores Lake and down a last lock of the same name. Then we are on the Pacific level, and a few miles further on we draw up and tie to the wharf at Panama itself, or Balboa as it is called.

We entered Colon Harbour at 1 p.m. and tied up at Balboa at about 8 p.m. It gets dark now always at 6 p.m., so the last two hours we did not see much. Difficult as it is to believe, we were tired out with the keenness of watching everything, and to add to it my lip was so painful I could hardly contain myself. The girls, too, were off colour and then another addition to the depression of all these factors was the cable to tell us of the sad news of the death of the old doctor. Kismet. Rain had ceased during the last part of the trip and we tried hard to join in the bustle and excitement of landing, but failed miserably. Leaving the others on the ship, I took Mum and Bynk on shore for a leg-stretcher and to see what we could see. Mum was, as usual, the best when there's any trouble about.

A road at Balboa Heights, c1916

We walked in the dark along a gorgeous motor road lit by electric lamps, while motors went by by the dozen. We all felt so miserable that we hardly had any experiences worth recording. A few fire-flies and a great hum of insects, and a steamy sweat. We were back in an hour and spent a night on board in a bath of perspiration. I am sure both the girls have lost several pounds weight already.

Friday, 5th October

Today has been undoubtedly the red-letter day of the whole trip. Of course we were tired after the stew-pot of last night, but it was now or never if we were to see the country. I got out off the ship with Val and Jon about 6-45 a.m. We went along the wharf meeting types of the population, Yankee police and Canal Officials, Blacks of all degrees of colour, from a bit of coal to the half-way mark of the half caste. The wharves and little patch of waste land held more than a sufficiency of interest for the boys for the all too short one and a half hours till breakfast time.

Gorgeous butterflies, reminding us of Mr. Grist's collection 'let loose.' Then the birds. Great scavenger buzzards, pelicans and curious stork-like things floated about in great numbers, whilst many beautiful smaller fry were all over the place. We learned that the boat would leave at 3 p.m., so that we had to get busy if we were to see the place properly. The tide was low and we could see boils in the water taking place continually, a sign of the eternal warfare of the finny race chasing, gobbling and being chased and gobbled. The boys and I felt it a fearful sacrifice to have to go sightseeing with the girls, but it had to be done from our duty to ourselves and also them. So we turned sorrowfully away from the water side. A large iguana, about two and a half feet, scuttled round some stones and muchly excited the boys, who longed for their catapults to go hunting.

I have forgotten to record that the fog had all cleared away and the 'Committee' had given us a glorious fresh morning of blue sky and brilliance. We arranged with a native to let us have a boat to go out and fish, if we got back in time, and that quieted the boys. Breakfast at 8 a.m. on board and at 9 a.m. we started to DO Panama. Mum and Bynk were feeling better and so we really set out to enjoy things.

We hired an automobile (a beautiful six-cylinder Yank, nearly new), driven by an American garage proprietor's wife, a Mrs. Persons, who was like our old friend Siddie Taylor.

Canal Zone residences, c1916

She was a splendid driver and as charming as some American women can be. Our party consisted of Mum, Bynk, myself, Val and Jon and also we asked a Mr. Hughes of N.Z. and two other ladies, a Miss Horne and another Miss Hill, to join up and halve the auto expense. First we drove round the residential quarters of the Canal Zone Officials and American Army Officers. It is very hilly all round and the houses and gardens are all most beautifully laid out. Hardly a leaf fallen or bit of rubbish anywhere. The whole district was as tidy as John Millburn's garden.

The road wound about until it reached the 'Administration Building' or Government Offices, situated near the top of the hill, about 250 or 300 feet high. From the terrace here the whole panorama of the district lay spread out like a map. All this residential suburb had been carefully and thoughtfully planted and laid out with every kind of tropical tree and flowering curiosity imaginable, like Kew Gardens. Then beyond lay the Canal disappearing back into the jungle whence we had come, and looking the other way, the entrance to Balboa Harbour with its jungle-covered hills and bays and island looking most beautiful as they fall to the shore of the Pacific Ocean.

Canal Zone, c1916

We then went for a drive of about nine miles out to
Old Panama, which is full of interest from historical
associations. An old ruined cathedral, a bridge over which
the great Morgan had to fight his way a few hundred years
ago. A few palm trees, a few native huts and a dense jungle
all around and the sand of the sea shore complete the
picture. We spent an hour here – all too short. Father
and sons butterfly and iguana hunting and getting stung
by pricklies. The others wandering amongst the ruins
and reflecting.

Back into the auto again, the drive was most helpful in partly
cooling us off. I feel we are really first class trippers today,
doing exactly what everybody else does, who has just a few
limited moments of call here. After nine miles back again to
the town of Panama, as distinct from Balboa, our lady
chauffeur took us to see her house, a pretty little bungalow
a couple of miles out. A tame monkey came out riding on
the back of an old mongrel retriever and jumped on to us
all in the car and was very friendly. We were presented by
Mrs. Persons with a bag full of lovely limes for future use
and some enormous bananas about 18 inches long.

Now we drove round New Panama town, which teemed with interest. The population of Panama is about 70,000. All sorts, Yanks, British, Spanish, half castes, Negroes, Chinks, Japs, etc., etc. There is a Chinese Quarter. The harbour with its fleet of native sailing craft of all sorts and sizes was worth an hour's study alone. The market, chiefly tropical fruits, was interesting in the extreme. I went and bought some of my beloved pawpaws and sweet plantains and mangoes for future reference on our ship.

The money here is of course American. I got a couple of pounds changed last night at the rate of 4.50, but as I was paymaster today for the party, I found it necessary to change a £5 New Zealand note into dollars. A coloured gentleman offered to give me 4.25 for it. (I thought of course 4.25 for each pound, which was a quarter dollar robbery on each pound) so said "O.K." and presented him with my fiver. He gave me 4.25 dollars and behaved as though the transaction was completed. A heated argument followed, of course, and I was very glad of the moral and bodily support of Mr. Hughes, and between us we managed to clearly show our coloured artist that the only alternative to an immediate return of my fiver, or five times as much American money, was a 'thick ear' or a hell of a disturbance. Result – immediate return of the New Zealand fiver. This money changing business is quite a nuisance when one is only making a short stay in a foreign country.

We now drove back to the ship and paid off our Lady Jehu. Just a bite was bolted and the girls spent the last hour in the vicinity of the ship while I took the boys to try for some sea fish. We got a boat and rowed out a bit, but did no good, of course, as we only had three-quarters of an hour and could not go to the place where it was good. We had also missed the tide. If I were travelling this way again, I would arrange to stay at Balboa for a week. The sea fishing is really good.

Back again on board, and by 3-15 p.m. we had pulled out and were heading out for the Pacific and the long dull reach of our journey.

S.S. *Remuera* in the South Pacific

I have omitted to record fully, for the last four or five evenings, the glorious lightning displays we have been treated to. My little Aneroid barometer went very low about the period of our entrance to the Caribbean Sea. Tonight was the big show and few realised what we were in for. When we came out after dinner it was, of course, pitch dark and our little party found a quiet corner and 'watched the lightning in the sky.' We seemed to notice that the flame was a different colour to the Atlantic lightning. There was a storm some miles off on our starboard and another a long way ahead of us, whilst all along the port side, quite 7 or 8 miles off was a great long irregular ragged lot of cloud bank, of course invisible except when the flares lit up different reaches of it. Some of it was blue, other great flashes were golden and at times the whole sky was lit up with a lurid yellow glare, blinking for seconds together. It was so far off that it was like looking into Heaven at times, and others resembled Dante's inferno pictures. The sea was quite calm and there was no breeze that would cool the air at all.

The usual deck-sleeping crowd came up and arranged beds, Elsie and Bynk bagging the end corner of the women's side, whilst I had the end corner of the men's so could communicate if necessary.

We all got off to sleep at about eleven and were waked up at 1 a.m. by the most awful storm I have ever been in. No wind – only rain in a solid wall, with lightning that poured out of the sky in rivers of flame and a noise that seemed as though it would split your ears open. It was blinding, terrifying. We remained up on the covered deck through it all and the ship's siren went booming all the time. The rain really was like a wall of water and the ship had to go quarter speed as nothing could be seen ahead through the deluge. The ladies had all to scoot off as the rain for a short space at the start, blew hard in their side. Mum and Bynk dragged their beds near mine, which was in a sheltered corner and we sat it out. Quite a lot of people had 'the wind up' properly. Val and baby were the only ones who slept through it. Jon was in the bunk over Val and was awakened, also Laura, but were not scared. They were really very good. That awful siren really is a terrifying thing though.

It was much cooler after 3 a.m. and we all got a doze after that, but I could see the glimmering of occasional flashes through my closed eyelids and several blankets. The thunder grumbled itself to sleep and the noise of our engines under us drowned all distant rumbles.

Saturday, 6th October

After last night's pandemonium, people are a bit lazy today. It is a calm sea and cloudy and raining hard all morning. Under the covered deck the different events of the sports are proceeding. A dull boring day.

Sunday, 7th October

Much about the same as Saturday, but weather gone quite cool. Have no thermometer but have had to discard white ducks and put on tweed or flannel. Cloudy sky, smoothish sea, temperature must be barely 70°. It is amazing, as we cross the equator about tea-time. Great hymn-singing all day and noisy yelling kids. Am very irritable. Wouldn't do for Jep to be here.

Monday, 8th October

Woke up after a good night in cabin. Still cool. Blankets on you in cabin with door shut is a marvellous contrast in a few hours from sweating on deck with no covering at all. One can hardly realise that only 300 miles away on our port beam is Guayaquil the seaport of Ecuador and then a few miles back from the coast are Chimborazo, Ilimani and the huge mountains of the Andes, running up over 20,000 feet.

We have not seen the sun since we left Panama, but we are sure to pick up the heat again before long. My lip has been most painful and must have been a disgusting sight, but this morning, thanks be, the heat has gone and it will be right in a couple of days.

We learn that the cool spell of weather is caused by winds that sweep down from the Andes to just this region and a cool current in the ocean that runs up between the Galapagos Islands and South America.

A very dull day again today, the usual deck sports, etc.; one splash of excitement was caused by a school of whales doing quite a lot of spouting. They were Orcas or Great Killer Whales. This great beast is the terror of the ocean and will kill the Giant Squid family. Quite different from the Greenland oil fellow.

We had a dance this evening started by the first class, who formally invited the second, but oil and water won't mix and I got quite a lot of fun as a looker on. I always feel annoyed at this dance mania performance as I cannot be of any service to our girls, who I fear don't get as much fun as if I was in the dancing clique. Shall be heartily glad when this monotonous voyage is through.

Postcard view of a section of the first class lounge, SS *Remuera*

Tuesday, 9th October

Yesterday, the sun came again about 11 a.m. and it got a little warmer then, but today it is very dull again and still weather for flannels and not white ducks. Val won the sweep on the day's run, 345 miles.

Whilst the dance was on last night I was introduced to a Mr. Wilson, a first class passenger, who is the proprietor of the *Auckland Weekly News* and resident of Auckland and evidently a power in the land. He is quite nice, a typical Colonial and willing to give a helping hand. I understand from him that there are one or two English Hoo Hahs going out to fish for trout, but he says they are such big pots that they can find things out for themselves. One is a peppery looking old ogre. A Colonel Bumscratcher or some such name. Wilson says he is the sort who would do their best to put anyone off where to go rather than help them. I rather hope I meet one or two of them in the future. Have met their sort before and generally get some fun out of them.

We are getting tired of this ship now. Poor menu and absolute indifference to whether passengers are satisfied or not. Many people are disgusted with this N.Z.S.Co. This boat is the best of the fleet and seems an excellent comfy sea boat, but there you have finished. Never again for me this route. The trouble is that they have no competition on this run and carry a big cargo. Passengers are a secondary consideration.

Wednesday, 10th October

From a weather point of view this has been about the most beautiful kind you can have in the tropics or elsewhere. Temperature about 75°, a light, gentle soft breeze from slightly to port side and a brilliant yellow burning sun, directly overhead at noon. A little movement on the boat, just enough to let you know you are at sea. After the melting swelter of the Caribbean Sea it is great. There the temperature was in the nineties, we have heard, for several days on end. I have been unable to be in touch with a thermometer this trip, but shall remedy that coming home.

There has been a big sports programme on all this afternoon. The girls went and took part and seemed to enjoy it, but I preferred seclusion and read in a corner on the foredeck. Only 14 more days, as the boys say when the term draws near the end, thanks be. I feel like a bird in a cage on this ship. There is no privacy at all.

We shall call at Pitcairn Island about next Tuesday and it will be a very welcome break. This lonely island, thousands of miles from anywhere, has a very remarkable history. The following little book should be read: *The Romance of Pitcairn Island*, by Fullerton, published by the Carey Press, 19, Furnival Street, London. We secured a copy temporarily and read it with great interest. Lip now better.

The Romance of Pitcairn Island

W. Y. FULLERTON

Thursday, 11th October

Same old uninteresting programme, all day. Nothing to do and plenty of time to do it in. Thanks be for our little family party. I have been told we are envied for our unanimity. We are mostly always together. If anyone gets temporary 'pip,' the others soon drive it away. Father is the only really unsociable bear. I really think, though, that if I did not go late into meals and emerge at the earliest possible moment, I should tear the table cloth off and heave bananas at the principal mugwumps around. Sometimes I feel as though I must shout or let off steam and the repression is most trying.

Concert tonight began 7-30. Couldn't stand the idea of it, so left Mum to perform a song to the rotten accompaniment of the flat flapper and cleared off to the foc's'le. There one felt in a world thousands of miles away from the rest of the ship; out of all reach of sound and vibration of the engines, one looked down at the prow of the ship cutting the black water in a soapy wave of foam. A new crescent moon hung low and the spirit of illimitable space filled one's whole personality. It was too early in the night for the Southern Cross to be visible, but the brilliance of the heavens generally was wonderful.

I was awakened from my reverie by the tong, tong of the bell on the bridge, two bells, then the answering tong, tong from the watch in the bows near me and the cry of "All's Well." In a moment "Aye, Aye" from the bridge and then the great silence again. I turned away and walked back from the things that matter and passed into the human part again.

First view – dining saloon of the first class. Mugwumps and puffy Hoo Hahs all belly-filling, dressed immaculately in black evening dress according to the dictates of their order. Females bejewelled and powdered and a stale smell of food oozing from the port holes (I had had my dinner). After passing this I felt inclined for nothing other than bed and sleep so make for cabin just as concert is finishing.

Friday, 12th October

A day of beautiful weather but no interest, so read most of the time and thought of all the old pals at home, particularly of you all at Cheylesmore, worrying out how you are going to get through the stuff in time, which is the never ending worry of a happy and successful printery. I felt quite a longing to call in this morning and hear all about it. There is rather a heavy swell running today, with a big heaving move on the ship. We are full of thanks really, that the voyage has, up to date, been on the very good side, but I should really like to see some of that calm extreme stillness one hears so much about, though I feel that if we were to enjoy much of that we should also have to pay and bring with it some of the hurricane weather, so let's be thankful and don't grumble.

Saturday, 13th October

Last night, after dinner, we were all lolling about on the foredeck and the 3rd Officer (Beautiful Bertie) was with us telling stories of wartime experiences (he was on a destroyer in the North Sea) when I noticed the young moon, which should be on the starboard bows, swing round over the bows slowly until she lay on our port quarter. Every few minutes engine bells kept tinging on the bridge above us and I felt nervous. We could feel that the engines had stopped and we seemed to be drifting aimlessly about. It was a temporary mechanical breakdown to the steering gear. (Thanks be that there was no sea on) and in half an hour all was well again, and at 8-15 p.m. the Captain gave another lantern lecture, this time on Pitcairn Island and its history. It was very interesting, but I could not sit still for more than about a third of it, so went to bed.

I woke up at 10 p.m., when the others came down, and had some tea they brought me and paid for it with a bad night. There was a shocking roll on the ship and I had a sort of premonition that it would get worse and was fidgety again.

Sure enough, at 1 a.m. the Night Watchman came round to the cabins and said, "Port holes to be closed, it's going to blow and rain hard." Felt miserable and cursed, though all the others were sleepy and happy. The scud soon passed and my barometer showed a wee rise from steadiness and today is a beautiful fresh morning again and the nightmare passed. It has been another glorious day of small fleecy cloud and dazzling sun brilliance.

Suppressed feuds and factions and love affairs, etc., are becoming more obvious. Likes and dislikes among the passengers are becoming more obvious. Thanks be, we can keep out of 'em.

We get about an hour most days or evenings and go through our repertoire of glees. Mum and Bynk take the two top parts and Val and I fill in the blanks to the best of our ability. 'A Wife's Song,' 'The Rainy Day,' 'Allan Water,' 'Number One John Braddleum,' are our star turns, with an odd hymn or two, all unaccompanied of course, as there is not a soul that has come forward that can play a simple accompaniment. What an absolute God-send Aunty Turb would have been to us, or Madge. I think we miss music more than anything.

Sunday, 14th October

Now we are in 'the Trades' and for several days the wind has been on our Port quarter in varying intensity, but the weather is really gorgeous. Officially it is quoted all these days as moderate breeze and moderate sea. A moderate sea has white horses, little ones, and if there's a swell with it, as there nearly always is in the middle of these vast wastes of ocean, there is considerable movement on the ship, but not enough to cause unpleasantness when you have your sea legs, as all have by now. Nothing exciting and nothing of interest to report. Mum sang 'But the Lord is Mindful' for Anthem at evening service.

Monday, 15th October

Another gorgeous day with a more scorching sun than ever. Most of the nuts and would-be nuts are making fancy dresses for a big 'do' on Wednesday night. Great interest centred on Pitcairn matters just now, as we should sight the island about dawn tomorrow and at 8 a.m. we should drop anchor about a mile off-shore. No women are allowed to go ashore and only a few athletic young men. I have put down my name and Val's in case there is any chance.

It appears there is a risk about it as you have to climb down the side of the ship on a rope ladder and get into a small boat that rises and falls perhaps 6 or 8 feet on the swell. Then a mile row and an exciting ride through the big curlers that roll up eternally on these lonely island shores, however smooth the sea may appear to be. (If the swell is heavy our Captain will not allow anyone to go.) You can never tell what it will be like, as only this afternoon a big heaving has developed from the southward. No white horses but great rolling mounds of water a mile across and perhaps 8 or 12 feet difference in level between hollow and summit.

Tuesday, 16th October

Before it was light, in the grey of dawn quite a few were astir to get the first view of Pitcairn. I went up with the boys for a look-out about sunrise, but we were too early. It was rather a stormy sky, and a bit fiery, but the sea was smooth enough except for the big heaving swell. I did not like the look of a dark, foggy haze directly in our course, which quite obscured our view for more than four or five miles. In fact, instead of seeing the island on a brilliant sunny morning, as we had hoped, at a distance of about 40 miles, we got within 10 miles before we saw it dimly through the fog. The gloom came towards us and heavy rain came down and obliterated everything, and the ship's engines stopping caused a silence that made us realise we were there.

Pitcairn Islanders prepare to board the *Remuera* (1916)

Postcard view of a Pitcairn Island photographed from a steam ship

About two miles off we could see the island that has such a romantic history. We had finished breakfast and were all up on deck awaiting developments. The disappointment over the weather was great. It meant little or no photography and priceless opportunities lost.

Our ship had stopped about one and a half miles away and through the rain we could see three sailing boats and one row boat coming out to the ship. It was most exciting. These poor souls had been waiting for weeks for this fete day and were bringing fruit and curios to sell. Only two or three times a year do they get news of the outer world, so one can hardly realise the excitement for them all. At last they were alongside and nearly all the population of the island had come and swarmed up the ladders like monkeys with baskets full of their produce for sale.

You must read *The Romance of Pitcairn Island.*

The rain now cleared up and although everything was wet the decks were like a village fete after heavy rain on a bank holiday at home, slippery with banana skins and orange peel. The atmosphere had cleared and visibility was quite good, but we badly wanted sunshine. A great hub-bub and excitement now held sway. I have never seen such unspoilt simple folk. They had not the slightest idea of values, but I think the majority of our passengers realised this and behaved generously. The two fellows we had on board, Warren and Christian, must have been great heroes. These simple folk are actually descended from the survivors of the mutineers of the *Bounty*, who took some women from Tahiti. There is very little sign as yet of in-breeding, but new blood will have to be imported soon to avoid degeneration. The people are dark-skinned, but not much so, perhaps about like Portuguese, and they talk English.

I felt far from well today and funked the trip ashore. No women were allowed although Bynk bearded the Presence in his bally caboose, but could not get sanction. Only about a dozen went. It was not a question of room for the crowd, but the job was to make up a boatful of passengers. I felt a nervous wreck after two or three bad nights and had not the guts of a rabbit, and felt that if I went I should make a fool of myself. There were only three would go out of the whole lot of second class passengers. An old Scotch hard nut and our Padre, Mr. Ledger and young Val, who was mad to go. The rest of the boat load was made up of a few first classers and some Marconi men.

I did not mind the rope ladder business, but I did mind what I could see in the distance. Great green combers roaring and bursting into tremendous surges as the swells hit the shore. Even with the glasses one could hardly make out any place where a boat could possibly land. I had recollections of crossing the reef years ago, in Ceylon, in catamarans and the experience is at least nerve racking.

They went over and down the rope ladder all right and we watched the little boat getting smaller and smaller. Then with the aid of the glasses I made out the boat engulfed in a splutter of spray and for a few anxious moments it had to all appearances been eaten up by the sea god. Then a little later we saw it thrown up on to the shingle of a tiny narrow beach only a few yards wide and Val had landed at Bounty Bay, Pitcairn Island. How I envied him or rather how I cursed myself that I could not carry on with him. The number of white men that have ever landed there can almost be counted on your fingers. Our Captain says that the *Remuera* is the only boat that calls there and only once before have any passengers been allowed to land. One can easily understand that a ship may call many times and the surge would make landing impossible.

Pitcairn Islanders in their longboat, photographed by Henry Keyse

Val shall now take up the story himself:

"When the time came for us to go ashore we had to go down the rope ladder and take our places in the boat, which was not a nice job, as the ladder wobbled all over the place. At last we pushed off from the *Remuera* and started rowing for the shore, six natives rowed with a big oar. The waves which had looked like round hummocks from the big ship, now looked like huge mountains and our little boat was tossed about like a cork. At last the land enclosed us and we found ourselves entering 'Bounty Bay.' We finally slowed up outside the line of breakers, which we now had to cross, and the steering oar

The dangerous waters of Bounty Bay, Pitcairn Island

was taken in and the rudder put out. We were finally ordered to different places to keep the balance right and told to hold tight. We now went very slowly forward waiting for a big wave to carry us over the breakers. At last a favourable wave came up behind us like a big green mountain, shooting us forward, and suddenly we found ourselves in fairly shallow water, behind us some treacherous looking rocks, over which was coming another huge wave, which broke against the boat, giving us all a free shower-bath, but before the next wave came up we heard a grating on the sand, and the boat

The landing, Bounty Bay, Pitcairn Island

was beached. We jumped ashore and were immediately greeted with welcomes from the Islanders who were left on shore and had come down to meet the boat. The landing stage is merely a framework of poles, and up the beach a few boat-houses consisting of a thatched roof on poles, in which are the canoes that the Islanders use for fishing in, when the weather is calm enough.

Looking down on Bounty Bay, Pitcairn Island

The S.S. *Remuera* photographed from Pitcairn Island by Henry Keyse

The people led us up to a steep muddy path, which was very slippery after the early rain; on each side of it grew tall palm trees, dense undergrowth and a few flowers. About a hundred yards up the path we came out on a steep rocky bluff from which we could see the *Remuera* in the distance. As we ascended the path more people (chiefly women and children) met us and welcomed us the same as the others had done.

The dogs are a funny looking lot of mongrels, quite friendly, but regard you as strangers and keep a watchful eye on you. At last, having gone over a fairly steep hill we came to 'Adamstown,' which is situated in a hollow between the hills; it is merely a number of huts with thatched roofs, only a few having corrugated iron ones. The church is the only two-storied building in the town. One of the women took Mr. Maclellan and myself into her house and gave us an orange each.

The houses are made very simply, consisting of a porch, behind that a passage with a bedroom leading off each side, it then opens out into a long living room, it then closes into a passage again, with two more bedrooms and another door. The furniture of the living room consists of a long table with benches and low chairs; there are photographs and beads, etc., hanging on the walls. Food, etc., is stored in outhouses.

Adamstown stands at the top of a steep hill. Photograph by Henry Keyse

When we had finished our oranges we went to the cemetery, down a path among groves of orange trees – each name has a line of graves, there are long lines of Christian and Young and McCoy, the three most common names in the island. We then went to John Adams' grave, which is by itself right away

The oldest known postcard from Pitcairn Island, written in 1906, shows young Ruth Constance Petch (born 11th July, 1898) next to John Adams' gravestone

Pitcairn's two story church photographed by Henry Keyse

from the others. In the distance we could see Adams' Cave*
with some wild goats by it.

It was time to go back to the ship. One lady gave me a big
basket of oranges and another some beads and a box made
out of a cocoanut. Two boats were launched, one carrying
fruit and Islanders went on in front, and the other with the
passengers. Going against the breakers was much easier than
going with them, as the tide was full and just on the turn, and
we were soon through, thank goodness.

We then hoisted our sail and went along easily until we were
level with the ship, then the sail was taken down, in which
proceeding we were all buried in canvas, and we went
broadside with the swell. One Pitcairn lady, who was in our
boat was sick, but we soon came alongside and got up on
deck. It was a bit worse going up the rope ladder now as all
the weight being on one side of the ship made the top of the
ladder overhang the bottom part.

I did so wish I could have caught some of the enormous
butterflies that I saw, but I had no net and there was only time

---

*This is an error by the young author, as the cave is actually known as
  Christian's Cave, after Fletcher Christian

for a quick run round. I should like to stop the whole of our holiday on the Island and make a collection of natural history specimens. The only birds that we saw were about as big as a thrush and the same colour, only without the spots on its breast. The only animals are harmless lizards and rats."

Main Road, Pitcairn Island, photographed by Henry Keyse

It took about an hour after the landing party had returned to collect up and despatch all the Islanders. Their parting was quite pathetic and many a tear and expression of emotion was to be observed on our decks as these lonely folk rowed away singing their farewell hymn to us. Cheers and good-byes and our engines started, and away we went on the last lap of our journey and looking aft, the little lonely rock grew fainter and fainter until it sank below the horizon and we were again alone on the waste of waters.

A selection of photographs showing passengers in their fancy dress costumes. Although taken on the *Remuera*, the date of this voyage is not known. Henry Keyse' advertising card, illustrated on page 30, states that he has materials for fancy dress available for passengers from his Hairdressing Saloon

Wednesday, 17th October

Most of the time last night was taken up in reviewing yesterday's interesting happenings. Now, today, the only thing has been the talk and preparations for the Fancy Dress Ball to be held tonight. A fusion of the first and second class, with an extension of time till midnight. The show promised to be a great success.

Mum was the moving spirit of our crowd in the organisation, etc., and all went well till 10 p.m., when the dance was drawn to a sudden end by a horribly sad accident. One of our passengers, a Mr. Tickell, who had a splendid war record in the navy, had got himself up in the garb of a Cannibal Chief. He wore a girdle of tow matting and was complete with spear and large meat bone to gnaw. He had greased his whole body coal black. A ragged-looking wig of brown tow covered his head.

Most of the people had come up on to the promenade deck, which was gaily decorated with flags, and were chatting and smoking, when Tickell asked someone for a match to light his cigarette. The flame of the match caught his tow girdle and the poor devil was enveloped in a sheet of flame.

The whole business only took about 15 seconds, but before a few calm and collected ones could get him down and the fire out, he was terribly burned. He was wearing an old pair of khaki shorts to cover his vitals. (The pair Stanley Saunders had lent to me) and that fact doubtless saved his life.

There was a slight panic amongst a few hysterical women, before quiet was restored and the patient carried off to the hospital on a stretcher.

Everybody went off to bed feeling very 'down' of course. (Note: Three days later he was reported to be very restless and not entirely out of danger, but his magnificent physique and constitution should bring him through all right.)

Thursday, 18th October

A dull uninteresting day. Nothing to record. Am getting bored to death. We played F.T. and F.R., etc.

Friday, 19th October

From 6 a.m. onward the weather has taken a bad turn. A gale from our starboard quarter has sprung up and we are officially charted 'Very rough sea, moderate gale.' The ship is plunging about badly, but nobody seems to mind except myself. Several intrepid spirits tried an airing on the forward main deck, but soon returned after being rolled over and wet through. I find the best place is cabin and a book. Our lot are all O.K. and apparently enjoying it.

Since we left Pitcairn, which is just south of the tropic of Capricorn, we have suddenly jumped into cool temperatures. All white uniforms and thin clothes have vanished and English winter clothes again donned. We are due at Auckland about next Thursday.

We hear that we are in touch by wireless with the S.S. *Rotorua*, the sister ship to this, now some days out from Auckland, homeward bound, and that she is experiencing very bad weather. That's cheering!!! How I hate all this turmoil. You can't stand or sit, and I can't even sleep with the racket. I have just looked at my little glass which has gone down badly at bed time. I think it has touched bottom and though still rough there looks a hope for the better.

Saturday, 20th October

Another miserable rough day. Sleep or semi-stupor in cabin all day. Can't keep warm. Even little Jon said "Dad let's shut our port and get up a good fug." The suggestion was unanimously adopted.

Poor Tickell, the cannibal chief, succumbed to his injuries and died at 8 p.m. – and so to bed.

Sunday, 21st October

Glass rising, thanks be, but weather chilly and sea with a foul swell on after the gale of Friday. It must have covered an extensive area. Cabin and fug again most of day for all of us.

At four-thirty p.m. all went for'ard for the funeral service of poor Tickell. I was never at a more impressive scene in my life. I do not think there was a dry eye amongst us, especially after the body had been consigned to the deep and the Last Post was

S.S. *Remuera* flying Nelson's signals in the South Pacific, year not known. Vice-Admiral Horatio Nelson died on 21st October, 1805

called on the bugle. If there was, it would be found amongst the officers and a few naval men of whom the deceased belonged.

The naval men and a few of the ship's people formed three sides of a square, leaving the side open to the sea, then dear old Mr. Ledger read the service most beautifully and the bearers carried the body to the side. The weather had dropped to a dead calm and the engines stopped during the short quarter of an hour service. You could have heard a pin drop.

It really has been an awful tragedy. A magnificently made young fellow about 28, with a fine strong clean open face, struck down in a scene of gaiety, and all was over in less than half a minute. He hardly recovered consciousness and was most frightfully burnt. Kismet.

Monday, 22nd October

Although cool it has been a perfect day, sea for a couple of hours was like oil, with a gentle swell, too small to make any movement on the ship. 'They' can't even now leave us alone, as there is a wireless message to say that a N.W. Gale is 'at it' near Auckland. However, to bed and a peaceful night. Nothing to do.

Tuesday, 23rd October

Calm sea all gone. White horses and a strong N.W. wind, but my glass has not gone down yet. A few deck games are being played. The girls and Val have gone down into the engine room. Jon is a bit off colour, and funked the steep ladder.

Here are a few points I omitted to state after my trip. A ton of oil is burned in 20 minutes. We took aboard 2,800 tons at Panama. She does four miles to a ton of oil. The temperature today is, on deck about 60°, hottest part of engine room, 100°. They went into the refrigerating room, which was 40° of frost, and got their noses frozen.

Tonight has been a farewell meeting of the second class. It consisted of songs, speeches and prize distributions. The Captain was present and was quite affable. Tomorrow is expected to be our last day on board and tomorrow the last night. Weather at bed-time continues a bit bouncy but nothing to grumble at.

I have omitted to record the presence of several huge birds that have been following the ship now for days. Several authorities have pronounced them to be Albatrosses, but I certainly do not find them to look like the specimens I have seen in South Kensington. They are wonderful gliders and sail along with never a wag of wing. They occasionally alight on the water to investigate some flotsam or jetsam that is dumped overboard from time to time. They vary greatly in colour. White underside and brown all over upper side, some are white back and dark brown wing tips and are about six to nine feet at least in wing span.

Wednesday, 24th October

Quite an uneventful day spent in repacking up all our mullock. We are due at Auckland tomorrow morning so this will be our last night on board. Nothing to do and so to bed.

Auckland Harbour 599

Friday, 26th October

As we crossed the 180th Meridian last night we have missed out Thursday altogether and have gone straight into Friday. It is funny to think of you all having your evening meal now at 7-30 as we are getting ready for breakfast. Before 6 a.m. one of the passengers was out waking everybody up. It was a lovely morning, cloudless sky and not a breath of wind. Sea like milk. We were in the Hauraki Gulf and mountains visible and islands being passed constantly. My! how beautiful it all looks. We are aching to get on the job.

Wharves and Shipping, Auckland, N.Z.

By 9 a.m. breakfast was long over and we had come to rest about a couple of hundred yards off our quay. We were in the fairway of Auckland Harbour at last with the large suburb of Devonport on one side and the wharves and shipping and Auckland on the other. The sky had clouded up and all the brightness has gone. It is just like a dull April day at home, temperature about 60°, no wind. Very beautiful it all looks with plenty of colour. Green trees and woody patches, some beaches and some cliffs. Very similar to a view of Bournemouth if in a semi-circle, looked at from half a mile from shore. Houses chiefly wooden bungalows of one or two stories painted green and stone colour or red and stone colour. Ferry boats and launches dart around. It was boring until after 11-30, when we were pulled into the quay and all the landing formalities took ages, it seemed.

Then Bynk was left in charge to wrestle with seeing all the luggage transferred to the Customs' Shed, 14 packages and the black box!!! while Mum and I scouted off into the town

S.S. *Remuera* at Prince's Wharf, Wellington, c.1920
(there is also a wharf by this name at Auckland)

to the boarding-house district to find quarters. We found one called 'Bellevue' after sampling several at 15/- a day. This is a pretty little shanty and we have dropped into clover. We have a large room like a dormitory for all of us, and Laura and Skibosh have a little corner on an upper floor. The food is splendid and the beds are comfy and we have got the outfit at 8/- per day per head.

The landlord and his missis are Yorkshire people and 'nice and 'omely,' and seem anxious to please and glad to have us. There are about 8 or 10 other people in the house. Back to the ship and then Elsie carted the crowd 'home' per tramcar and Bynk and I stayed to see to the transfer of luggage. All was cleared and we were installed by 4 p.m.

It is now raining and blowing, as usual wherever I go, and we are feeling somewhat as though we would give a lot for a fire and our little snuggery at old Beechwood. Elsie, Bynk and I went down into town after dinner and went to the pictures. Raining hard, back home and so to bed.

Saturday, 27th October

It should be a matter of interest to record that I am disappointed in the fact that I have to wear my thick pants and vests as though I were at home. A nasty squally sort of day.

Have been down town and got films developed and am sending prints with this diary by Monday's mail. Am very fed up with the Kodak people in London. I hope Mr. Hewson will call and tell them of rotten service. They were supposed to see that my camera was in perfect order. The shutter mechanism has gone wrong and spoilt nearly half my pictures. Some were most interesting subjects and can never be got again. I am trying to get it repaired in Auckland.

Have been to see Mr. Farrell (the Standard Motor Agent) and have arranged with him for the use of a big 'Dort' car, a Yank, something like Cyril White's old 'hearse.'

From what I hear we are in for motoring of a kind that we never even have imagined. On the run down to Napier from here we are likely to ford creeks and be bogged up in mud axle deep. We have to take – a spade, a pulley block-rope, an axe and crowbar. Mr. Farrell is taking us all round for a drive this afternoon and tomorrow, Sunday, and then next week I must begin to get a move on.

Evening. Mr. Farrell took us about 25 miles in the Dort. All round the environs of Auckland. The weather was blustery, spring-like but bright. The car seated Elsie and Bynk, Laura, Jon and Baby in the back and Val and I sat in front with Farrell. We did several very steep bits of hills, which she did on second with plenty to spare. It's a 20 h.p. car and does about 20 to the gallon or 25 on a long straight run.

After evening meal, Mum and I had a walk down town and bought some bananas from Mr. Wong Chang, and then home and bed.

1918 advertisement for Dort Fourseason Cars (Wikipedia)

Sunday, 28th October

A lovely sunny May day, warm but a strong wind. Lounged about in the sun in a more or less sheltered corner of the park in front of this house. It is a sort of glorified 'Top Green,' five times as big and hilly, with wide asphalt walks and a monument or two and German guns, a flagstaff and most beautiful trees, shrubs and flower beds, scores of arum lilies grow everywhere and big magnolia trees. Palms and sub-tropical stuff seem to do well. The whole patch is high up and overlooks a lot of the town and harbour. Farrell took us for another drive round today, including a run in the car to the top of Mount Eden, the view-point of Auckland. We could see for 50 miles in all directions. Home and to bed. Must now wind up this section of Diary for Mail despatch tomorrow morning.

Monday, 29th October

Terrific rush this morning to get various packages for different people off for the mail, also landlord wishes to make structural alterations to our room, so has given us other (improved) quarters in the house. Crossed the harbour today from Auckland to Devonport; beautiful sunny day, fresh breeze. Auckland is really a magnificent town. Went in a few shops. Whitcomb and Tombs is like Burgis and Colbourne at Leamington, only a lot bigger and infinitely nicer and smarter. Also other shops. Lots of the town is very, very like Victoria, B.C. Hope to get car tomorrow. He (Farrell) says it would be a shame to use a 'Standard' for the sort of work I want to do on wheels, besides they are too much money for me out here.

1923

PITCAIRNERS VISIT LONDON
INTRODUCTION

Even to this day, Pitcairn is an extremely isolated island. However, thanks to the internet, the inhabitants are as up to date as the rest of us with the events taking place in the world about them.

A hundred years ago it was an entirely different situation. The only way that the Islanders could find out about the world was by speaking to the crew and passengers of ships that briefly called, by reading second-hand newspapers donated to them, or by their correspondence with friends and relatives abroad which sometimes took months to be delivered.

For that reason, the adventure of two Pitcairn men, Elliott Christian and Skelly Warren, organised by the British *Daily Mail* newspaper, made interesting stories around the world as you will see over the next few pages.

SAVOY THEATRE

Proprietors .. .. .. THE SAVOY THEATRE LTD.
Licensed by the Lord Chamberlain to RUPERT D'OYLY CARTE, Savoy Hotel, W.C.
Lessees .. .. .. The Executors of H. B. IRVING.
Under the management of ROBERT COURTNEIDGE.

THE MILBORNE SYNDICATE present

POLLY

Transferred from the Kingsway Theatre

SEE THE THEATRICAL COMPETITION ON PAGE 19.

Theatre programme for the 1923 production of *Polly*
at the Savoy Theatre in London

1923

"THIS LONDON"
15TH OCTOBER

Manawatu Daily Times

This newspaper article is reproduced from the *Manawatu Times*, New Zealand, with the kind permission of Stuff Limited (https://www.stuff.co.nz), and the National Library of New Zealand (*Papers Past* – https://paperspast.natlib.govt.nz).

Amazed Pitcairn Islanders
Praise for English Girls

The two Pitcairn Islanders, Elliott Christian and Skelly Warren, finished their two days' lightning tour of London recently by a visit to the theatre – another thing they had never done before. The two men, both married, are among the first to leave the lonely island in the Pacific since the mutineers of H.M.S. *Bounty*, from whom they are descended, founded a colony there 136 years ago.

The zenith of their ambition was reached when the *Daily Mail* provided them with a flight in an aeroplane. They had never seen aircraft before and when on visiting Croydon they saw the air liners arriving from Amsterdam, Paris, and Cologne they were clamorously excited to "go in the clouds."

The trip was all too short for their desire. On landing Warren very thoughtfully remarked, "This London! Why we could see no end to it; it must be bigger than the whole of Pitcairn!" (which measures one mile and a-half long by one mile broad).

Both men have an eye for beauty and were loud in their praise of the prettiness of English girls.

A visit to Marconi House, where a demonstration of wireless telephony was arranged for them and an intensive lesson in the operation of a receiving set which has been presented to the island by the Marconi Company, filled up the afternoon, and after visiting *Polly* at the Savoy Theatre, the islanders returned just before midnight to their fo'c'sle home in the New Zealand Shipping Company's liner *Remuera*.

The Auckland Star.

Table Talk
26th October

Two Pitcairn Islanders, who had been on a visit to England, returned to their island home by the *Remuera* on her present voyage out.

A passenger on the *Remuera*, Petty Officer Tickle, on his way to join H.M.S. *Philomel*, was fatally burned while taking part in a fancy dress ball on the vessel, and died last Saturday.

1923

SEEING LONDON
27TH OCTOBER

The Evening Post.

Pitcairn Islanders' big adventure
A memorable trip
(By Telegraph – special to *The Post*)
Auckland, This Day.

The passengers on the steamer *Remuera*, which arrived in Auckland yesterday, had more than the customary passing glimpse of Pitcairn Island and its lonely inhabitants, for the ship not only carried two of the islanders back from London, but also remained off the island for about seven hours, during the greater part of which time some thirty children from the shore were entertained on the ship. It was on the *Remuera*'s last trip Home that the two Pitcairn Islanders made the big adventure of their lives by leaving their lonely home and setting out to see the world, or at least the hub of the world, London. They were Messrs. Skelly Warren and Elliot Christian, who are well-known to those who have been at Pitcairn a few times.

When they got to London they had indeed the time of their lives. The *Daily Mail* adopted them, and they were taken everywhere. One day they spent at the Zoo, another day at the Tower and St. Paul's, and so on. They were even taken up in an aeroplane. Well-known chocolate manufacturers had them to their model villages, and loaded them with sweets. Some excitement and entertainment was provided for them throughout their stay.

They remained each night on the *Remuera*, and they were indeed sorry to say good-bye to their kind friends in London. When the ship at last sailed, however, they came away with huge packets of all sorts of useful articles, and had the satisfaction of knowing that there were no eagle-eyed Customs officials waiting for them at Pitcairn.

When the *Remuera* reached Pitcairn about daybreak there was great excitement among the islanders, who quickly came out in their boats laden with prime fresh fruit and the usual assortment of curios; but, in addition, the children were there, and they scrambled up on deck much to the delight of the passengers. Then the youngsters gave a concert, and for three or four hours off and on they sang most delightful melodies, sacred and secular. Everybody on board was charmed with the entertainment, and it was quite touching when the time came for these men and children to leave the vessel. When they were back in their sturdy little boats they sang 'God be With You till We Meet Again,' and the little scene proved very affecting as the big ship drew away.

The photograph on the right shows Pitcairners boarding the New Zealand Shipping Company's *Rangitane*

1924

ISLAND OF DREAMS
ARTICLE BY A RATHER GRUMPY MAN

This extract is from a long article, published in two Saturday editions of the *Waikato Times*. I have not included the author's description of the mutiny on the *Bounty*, or details of the first settlement on Pitcairn. I begin with T.C.L.'s description of Pitcairn in 1924.

Incidentally, I almost feel like apologising for including it here – I'm not at all surprised that T.C.L. did not give his full name in the newspaper! He seems to be a very jaded fellow, and despite his attempts at 'doing them down', in my opinion, the kindness of the Pitcairners still manages to shine through his disappointing words. I found it offensive, as I am sure the Pitcairners did at the time if they managed to obtain a copy of the article, that an entire race of people could be judged by just one person, and that person was almost certainly forced to do something that they did not want to do.

Having said that, there are parts of the article to enjoy, so please try to read behind the lines and ignore the extreme grumpiness of T.C.L.

PITCAIRN ISLANDERS

A group of four Pitcairners, photographed by Henry Keyse.
Left to right: John Lorenzo Christian (born 1895), Burnett Stanhope
Christian (born 1897) Cora Christian, and her husband, the island
magistrate, Robert Elliot Christian. The three men were brothers.

1924

ISLAND OF DREAMS
7TH & 14TH JUNE

The Waikato Times.

This newspaper article is reproduced from the *Waikato Times*, New Zealand, with the kind permission of Stuff Limited (https://www.stuff.co.nz), and the National Library of New Zealand (*Papers Past* – https://paperspast.natlib.govt.nz).

Life on Pitcairn
A Romantic History

Last chapter yet unwritten. Observations and impressions (By T.C.L.)

… today the island, being almost in the track of vessels running between New Zealand and Panama, is regularly visited and therefore kept in more or less close touch with the outside world. No vessel is more anxiously awaited than the *Remuera* and no one held in greater regard than Captain Cameron, whom they call 'Our Father.' And a good father he is to them. In fact he is a kind of Santa Claus. He brings them letters, papers, parcels and goods, and occasionally takes one of the men on a visit to England or New Zealand. No wonder they look up to him and regard him so benignantly.

First Glimpse of Island

It was early Sunday morn, March 30, when we got our first glimpse of the island. The sea was smooth and blue as it can only be in tropical parts. Far ahead could be seen a faint outline of land. As we came closer it took the form of the Saddleback, at New Plymouth, or Somes Island, at Wellington. The officers said we would arrive about 11 o'clock, and probably would meet there the *Ruahine* coming from Panama. Church service was therefore begun on the deck at 10.30 instead of 11. It was a unique scene – the vessel moving through the pellucid seas; flying fish and sharks (observable by their ugly fins) gamboling on either side, shepherding the boat as it were; land in the form of what appeared to be a conglomeration of rock arising abruptly from an illimitable expanse of water; a mixed congregation following the Church of England service presided over by a Nonconformist but assisted by Anglican clergymen (for there were eight or nine padres aboard), and singing such appropriate hymns as 'For Those in Peril on the Seas.' The backs of most of the congregation were to the island, and as soon as the short service concluded all eyes were turned towards the romantic isle. It was a picture in which the eyes feasted for many minutes. Instead of masses of rock one saw verdant patches, cocoanut and other tropical trees waving, and at the bottom, near the shore, clusters of people, ant-like in size from our distance.

"Will you see the *Ruahine*?" was the question. "Just around the corner!" answered an officer. Smoke arose, and everybody rushed off to get his or her letters, etc., ready to be posted for New Zealand. As we rounded the island, instead of the *Ruahine* we saw but a trail of smoke. The vessel had slipped on to the other side and was making for her destination. "A dirty trick!" exclaimed an irate lady from Taranaki, "they could easily have waited a few minutes longer and taken our letters and postcards!" The name of the captain of the vessel was taken in vain more than once by the indignant passengers, who talked of wirelessing their protest to him.

Impressions of the People

Meantime specs on the ocean began to assume the proportions of boats, heavily laden and strongly manned. They were the Pitcairn Islanders. Naturally, after the lecture given the previous evening by Captain Cameron on the Mutiny of the *Bounty* and the life of the Pitcairners, all were eager to ascertain what manner of men and women were the descendants of the mutineers. They found them totally unlike any other people. Of course they varied in type. One could see evidence of the Caucasian origin. Especially was this the case in connection with one named McCoy, a lineal descendant of the armourer or blacksmith, McCoy, who, were he set in different surroundings, would be regarded as a jovial-natured Hibernian. McCoy, by the way, is one of the rangatiras of the island. Then one remarked the refined and aesthetic features of one or two of the men, and it was not surprising to find they bore the names of Christian and Young. These, it was subsequently found, are the most common names on Pitcairn. Christian, of course, was the leader of the mutiny, and Young was a midshipman, both coming from leading English families. They are still known by their progeny. Some of the other islanders partook of the appearance of their maternal forebears, albeit there was apparent a sallowness betokening a tendency to T.B.

There was quite a number of island women in the boats, which now numbered three, and large ones they were, all made, we learned, by the islanders themselves and capable of holding forty persons.

The women were not altogether prepossessing, though there were exceptions. Their appearance was largely spoilt by their teeth, or want of them. Unlike the Maoris and other aboriginals, they have very poor teeth. Whether this is caused by a lack of lime in the plant and vegetable life or the water they drink, or is a legacy bequeathed to them by their paternal forebears, has not been defined. They have a dentist on the island. In size, he is the biggest man there, and called

Melville Christian. He has a set of primitive forceps, and his greatest pleasure, so it is said, is to use them. When an islander has toothache he promptly goes to Melville, who as promptly gets to work with the forceps. He believes in the frontal attack as affording the only effective remedy for teeth troubles. None of your stopping or crowning or bridging for him! Yank them out! A few trips ago Melville saw the *Remuera* surgeon and commissioned him to secure some cocaine, as his feminine victims were complaining of the pain attending the extractions. The surgeon, however, declined, feeling that Melville was already doing a good deal of harm and he did not desire to be an accessory to extending his opportunities for further mischief.

Three Pitcairn boats close to a visiting steam ship (real photo postcard)

Skill in Landing

But, back to the boats. Chattering like so many monkeys, some singing of the briny, others humming popular English airs, ropes were thrown to them from the ship, rope ladders put down, and with an agility born of long practice, and cumbered with baskets of fruit (more or less green), small work baskets, boxes, shell necklaces and other articles of their own manufacture, they negotiated the ladders and sprang aboard, and having made due obeisances to the captain and his officers, commenced selling their wares to indulgent and curious passengers. Oranges, looking far from appetising, though sweet and juicy, were offered at eight for a shilling; bananas, also green, at about the same price; coconut boxes with handles, 2s 6d; work-boxes made from native miro wood, from 10s to £1; little palm kits at from 1s 6d to 2s 6d. The prices were high for the values offered, but the buyers did not seem to mind.

Cargo was taken aboard the boats, including some boxes of clothing and books that had been collected by Mrs. C. H. Burgess, of the New Plymouth branch of the Victoria League, which the islanders took as a matter of course, and with no exuberant expression of gratitude, and those of the passengers going ashore were ordered to get into the boats as quickly as possible. The process was not as simple as it looked, as the range of the sea was fairly considerable, and one had to judge accurately and act quickly in order to escape being immersed in the sea or jambed between boat and vessel.

It is worth going ashore on Pitcairn if only to witness the skilful boatmanship of the islanders. On our boat, besides the crew of about twenty were twenty-three passengers, and it seemed to be dangerously low in the water. However, that was a trifle which appeared to give the boatmen no concern. As previously stated, there is no natural landing place on the island, which is exposed to the full force of the Pacific on every side. But, all the same, the islanders launch and land their boats quite safely. Their landing-place is between – or, rather, over – some big rocks. They wait for a big wave which takes them between and over the rocks, and then, by rapid rowing and backing, they turn at right angles and get behind some covering rocks, and then into smooth water and on to the skids.

At the landing seemed to be assembled the remainder of the island's inhabitants. They were the less virile and mobile. Old men, old women, young girls and boys, babies, the decrepit and the deformed. They were not a very impressive lot, save for the youngsters, who appeared to be much like the youngsters of a Maori pah, though perhaps better clothed and showing signs of being more cared for. They told an eloquent tale of Nature's penalties for breaking her consanguineous laws.

Journey to the Settlement

"Welcome to our home!" cried the women as they came to meet us. Shaking us heartily by the hand, they continued: "We are pleased you have been able to come and visit us." We were escorted to the boatsheds made of local timber and the leaves of the plantain. Here we were offered fruit in abundance. It was fiercely hot. The tropical sun poured down its rays, tempered by no breeze as on the boat, and the heat came up from the reddish-brown soil as well as from above.

To reach the settlement, 'Adamstown' (named after the last of the mutineers, John Adams) meant a climb up the cliffs of about a thousand feet. The track – it can hardly be described as a roadway – is cut for the most part through soft sandstone, and the gradient is in most places exceedingly severe, at least one in three. It would not involve a great deal of work to reduce the gradient and improve the track, but what was good enough for the original settlers is evidently good enough for the present-day islander, who has lost whatever capacity he ever had for work.

This was demonstrated on the plateau in which the village nestles. No defined plan for either paths or dwellings has been followed. The houses are dumped about anywhere, and the paths wind in and out of them. The village in some respects resembles Parihaka in its halcyon days, except that it cannot sport the two big, well-built buildings that were a feature of the last stronghold of the Maoris in Taranaki. The number of mongrel dogs and growls of hybrid breeds were also reminiscent of Parihaka.

The main pathway from the top of the hill to the village, is, however picturesquely lined with banana, coconut, pawpaw and mango trees, and festoons of climbing and creeping flowers, all charging the atmosphere with a rich tropical scent so potent in the heat as to render one almost sick.

Main Road, Pitcairn Island, photographed by Henry Keyse

The houses are built of island wood, with lining of American pine taken off a timber scow wrecked years ago on a tiny island some sixty miles away. The buildings are raised some four or five feet from the ground, as protection, one was told, against the depredations of the red and black ant. For the same reason tables, etc., are based on glass or metal canisters. The kitchen or eating room are detached from the main building, which, considering the extreme heat which obtains on the island, is as wise as it is necessary. The living room is in the centre and the bedrooms on either side, as is the case with the general run of beach cottages in our own Dominion. The furniture is not very elaborate, consisting of a single bed and box, and, in the dining and living rooms, of a table and form of chairs. The interiors are scrupulously clean, which is more than can be said of the exteriors, for in the space under the house the dogs and fowls seek protection from the sun and heat.

School and Church

The main building on Pitcairn Island is the combined church and school, the ground floor being devoted to religious purposes and the upper to teaching the young idea. The church room has accommodation for over 200 persons and is well lighted and ventilated.

Church service had been held the day before (Saturday), and the amount of the collection was written in a clear and strong hand on a blackboard, it being £9 7s 3d, which, considering the small population, testifies to their liberality and earnestness of faith. The schoolroom above is practically a replica of the church room. The teacher is generally the spiritual adviser.

Just outside and detached from the building is the church bell, which came originally from Kamassi, on the Gold Coast of Africa. It is used for warning the populace of the coming of a steamer and visitors that it is time to depart, as well as for calling the people to church and the children to school. It is, therefore, a very useful bell.

In John Adams' day, and for many a day thereafter, the islanders were adherents of the Church of England, but for the past thirty or forty years they have embraced the doctrines of the Seventh Day Adventists, who are generally represented on the island by a missionary.

Aboard the *Remuera* were a missionary and his wife who were to stay on the island for six months. The natives firmly believe that the end of the world is in sight, and are preparing, not to render themselves more useful and of more service in this world, but for the next. They eschew drinking, swearing and smoking. One of the party offered an islander, who was guiding us, a cigarette. "No, no; we don't smoke; it is not good for us." Neither do they read books except for those prepared for them by their spiritual advisers. Indiscriminate reading might make them too worldly.

Historic Cemetery

The cemetery is one of the chief points of interest whence you are led by the islanders. It is situated quite near the settlement, and all around it is thick tropical jungle, faced with heavily laden orange and lemon trees. The graves are evidently regularly tended. One island lady, a daughter of McCoy, referred to above, showed us the grave of her late husband, who, with two others, had been drowned in landing in the surf two or three years before. It was beautifully kept,

The Cemetery, Pitcairn Island, photographed by Henry Keyse

with fresh flowers in receptacles that did duty for vases. She appeared to be in no way cast down by the demise of her husband. Rather did her conversation give the impression that his was the happier lot. It is a comfortable philosophy. This lady had two children on whom she was bestowing her affections and leading in the right way. In colour and general appearance she was a regular Polynesian, and in the Dominion would invariably be taken for a superior type of Maori woman, yet her father, McCoy, possesses as white a skin as anyone.

Next we were taken to the grave of John Adams. It lies some distance away from the main cemetery, and here again tropical fruit trees surround and almost grow over the place, which is noted not only for being the last resting place of the last of the survivors of the *Bounty*, but because of the headstone, which was a gift of Queen Victoria, who was greatly interested in the story and life of the Pitcairners. It is a very old stone, of course, having been erected a few years after 1829, when Adams died, and shows that the old Queen could exercise the virtue of frugality on occasions of making such disinterested gifts. We were anxious to see the grave of Fletcher Christian, but were informed that he lay buried where he was shot with the others, higher up and some distance away, too far to negotiate in the time at our disposal.

As we proceeded to another part of the village we heard the strains of a familiar ditty. We listened and thought it was the islanders indulging in singing, but as we came through an avenue of large banyan trees we discovered that the vocal music emanated from a gramophone – the modern and the ancient, science and primitiveness cheek by jowl with a vengeance.

The banyan trees were of unusual interest to visitors mainly because of their roots obtruding from the ground. Instead of going downward the process is reversed, and they grow upwards, some to a distance of from 20 to 30 feet, the tree proper growing above that. How they withstand wind and weather is difficult to understand.

The pawpaw tree is also interesting because of its clusters of fruit emerging from the stem of the leaves, whilst the clusters of bananas drooping and bearing down the whole tree by their heavy weight was another object of interest.

No Need to Toil

Coconut trees reared themselves up more than twice as high as the tallest of our cyathias (tree ferns), but nearly in every case were bent by the prevailing winds. The islanders drink largely of the coconut milk, preferring it to that of the goat, which also provides the islanders with the only meat they get. We did not see the goats, which were grazing on the more inaccessible parts of the island, nor the only horse that they possess. One could pity the animal if it had to haul any loads up the steep track we were obliged to negotiate. There could be seen cherry, peach and apricot trees growing, like the lemons and oranges, entirely without attention on the part of the islanders.

One could not find any evidence of work on the island. Nature does her work so well in such a climate that man need not exert himself. He grows a few kumaras and taros, he catches fish (the waters of the island abound in edible fish) and fruit forms the rest of his diet. The only time he bestirs himself is when he launches his boat and goes off to a passing vessel to sell the fruit and articles collected and made by his spouse. He has solved the problem of the cost of living, and it can be understood that he casts no envious eyes on his white brother in other climes who by necessity has to hustle for a crust. But for this comfortable, languorous existence he has to pay, and the last chapter of the mutiny of the *Bounty* and life on Pitcairn Island has still to be written.

The visitor, with all the chief points of the romantic and interesting history of the island and the islanders in his mind, lands in the full expectation of meeting an unsophisticated people and to find conditions equalling those of Utopia, but he is soon disillusioned. In late years frequent contact with vessels and trading with passengers have made the Pitcairner nearly as materialistic and covetous as the Maori at Rotorua, and though as yet his religious affiliations and convictions have not weakened, there is judging from what one saw of their dealings, considerable scope for the practice of the virtues they profess. They have a growing appreciation of money and what it can do, and it is part of their education that could advantageously have been spared.

The Pitcairner has of late years developed a desire for corrugated roofing iron, which he is submitting for mango leaves with which most of the buildings were thatched. This enables him to catch and store the rain-water which hitherto escaped, making things at times very unpleasant. Recently a spring was discovered some distance away, so that the danger of a drought occurring is not so real as it formerly was.

The guttering of the houses is original, consisting of a coconut tree cut in half, whilst the down pipes are of the same material.

Island of Rich Soil

The soil on the island is extremely rich, appearing to be of a chocolate-coloured volcanic loam, strongly impregnated with guano. Anything could be readily grown on the island. One noticed patches of sugar-cane, and a small crushing mill, operated by manual or horse power, the juice being highly prized by the youngsters, which may be another cause of their bad teeth. No cereal is grown. The islanders obtain their flour from passing ships. They are strict tea totallers, only using spirits for medicinal purposes.

Among themselves they speak an English patois, cutting off terminals of words and running them into one another, and it is not easy for the outsider to ascertain their meaning. At first their speech appeared to resemble that of the Maoris more than English, but, on questioning them, it was found they had lost touch entirely with the Polynesian tongue. Which perhaps is not surprising for in the first days of the settlement the white men would no doubt teach the native women English as well as they could, it being fairly certain that they would not bother to learn the language of their spouses. The latter would not be able to pronounce the strange words fully, and so from that a language of their own would be evolved. One noticed that when speaking amongst themselves they used 'Pitcairnese,' but on addressing the visitors they would speak English clearly and intelligently, and, in some cases, quite fluently.

The islanders some time ago were given a wireless receiving set by a kinsman descendant of one of the original mutineers, and so they know of the approach of visiting vessels. But it is not contemplated that they will be entrusted in the near future with the sending apparatus.

Back to the Steamer

The bell clangs, and it is time to leave the plateau and make for the landing. By this time most of the visitors were perspiring freely, perspiration pouring down their faces, clothes hanging limply, and all developing thirsts that were not assuaged by liberal helpings of the succulent oranges – they contain twice or three times as much juice as the island oranges you buy in New Zealand – and the milk of the coconut. The natives lined the precipitous track to the boatsheds and cheered us on our way.

Before we were allowed to enter the boats we were 'tapped' for 10s apiece, the amount of the fare. It was interesting to watch the islanders start off. Heavy seas were pounding on the rocks behind which the boats were ensconsed. The boatmen watched their opportunity, and as soon as a wave spent itself with a wild cry pushed out their craft and soon were riding upon a huge wave. Sometimes the waves break and the water enters the boat. That was our experience, a wave drenching all and sundry, but it was not an unwelcome experience because all were feeling the effects of the intense island heat.

Still the boat was heavily laden and the pressure of a lot of water did not add to the safety of the voyage to the ship. The boats, however, are sturdily built, the islanders not having lost the art handed down from the mutineers. No one seemed to be in command, all jabbering together, and giving orders and counter orders, and it was well that nothing untoward happened, for they did not inspire confidence in their ability to meet an emergency. To catch hold of and gain a footing on a rope ladder from a rocking boat in the open, swelling sea was no easy task, and thankful were we all when at last the feat was safely accomplished. Coming on top of the torrid experiences on the island, it was little wonder that many were completely exhausted when they reached deck and made a beeline for their berths. All the same, it was a most interesting trip that none would have cared to miss.

The boat whistled, the islanders made their adieux, and scuttled down into their boats. Each rested on his oar, the women looked upwards, each coxswain gave his long stern oar a twist, and, as they started to drift towards their island home a mile and a-half distant, they sang, in sonorous accents, the old appropriate hymns, 'In the Sweet By-and-bye,' and 'God be With You till We Meet Again.' It was a clear, beautiful tropical afternoon, and the scene and the singing were such as were not likely to be forgotten by those aboard the good ship *Remuera*.

The Experiment Discussed

As the strains of the sweet vocal music became fainter and gradually died away as the vessel stood again towards the immense expanse of the Pacific, thoughts of the islanders and what was in store for them pressed uppermost in the mind.

Two Pitcairn boats close to a visiting steam ship

Here was a great and unique experiment – the planting on an island hundreds of miles off the navigators' beaten track of a small number of white men and Polynesian women, there to work out their destinies uninfluenced or unaffected by the outside world. That the white men and the brown men quarrelled and slew each other and the remaining whites in turn fell out with each other were of less consequence than the fate of their offspring and the physiological result of the union of white and brown. These aspects, of course, would probably not have been given much consideration by the mutineers.

Has the experiment proved a success? Can white and brown mix in equal proportions without harm to their physical and mental well-being? These questions are not difficult to answer.

It is recorded that Bishop Selwyn, when in charge of the Melanesian Mission, educated a Pitcairner, and subsequently arranged with a business man in Auckland to take the boy into his office. To his surprise and regret he found the boy a great disappointment; he had neither memory nor capacity. Really this result is not surprising. Where there is inaction there is atrophy. A limb unused for long soon becomes powerless, requiring considerable massaging and exercise before it will function again properly. It is the same with the mind. Unless it is exercised, given work to do and problems to solve, it soon loses power and capacity. Nothing is truer than the old saying that the less you do the less you can do, and conversely, the more you do the more you can do.

What of the Future?

The islanders have not seriously exercised their minds for generations and consequently cannot concentrate or perform mental tasks which offer no difficulty to the average New Zealand child. They are content to live their own way, and it is an easy and pleasant way. Two attempts to transfer them to other environment failed, and, after mixing with them, and seeing their manner of life, one can quite understand the reasons.

Physically the experiment has not been a success. Far from it. The islanders have deteriorated considerably from the standard of their forbears. Intermarriage has told its tale and unless new blood is introduced the days of the extinction – or worse – are not far off. As in the brute animal kingdom so in the human kingdom, persistent inbreeding lowers the stamina and undermines the powers of resistance, bringing in its train troubles both of the body and the mind.

Authorities tell us that after three generations of life in London families fail to reproduce themselves. It is Nature's penalty for disobedience of her laws. The islanders have plenty of sunshine and plain foods, indeed, everything that heart can desire, but they are disobeying Nature's laws in another and even more serious way, and they are suffering from the consequences in restricted fecundity, malformation, etc. Imbecility may form the next chapter of the history of the islanders unless sterility accomplishes its purpose before.

Group of young Pitcairn Islanders, photographed by Henry Keyse

The 1924-25 New Zealand national rugby team,
nicknamed *The Invincibles All Blacks*

The 1924-25 All Black tourists to the
British Isles and France were dubbed
'the Invincibles' because they won
every game.

(Wikipedia)

1924

ALL BLACKS DEPART

30TH JULY

The Evening Post.

Five Weeks' Voyage to Plymouth

The 1924-25 All Blacks have gone forth to play New Zealand's national game in the Old World, and from an unusual stir of over two months' duration there is now calm in the Dominion's Rugby circles, only, however, for the period during which the All Blacks will be en route to England. With news of their deeds in other lands, there will then come another great revival of interest. At the appointed hour – 4 o'clock – yesterday afternoon, the liner *Remuera* drew away from King's Wharf, carrying with her the All Blacks and official party travelling with the team. A brief stoppage was made in the stream, after which the liner put to sea, bound for Plymouth, where the All Blacks are to be landed, and then to proceed to Newton Abbott, their headquarters, for the tour.

The final scenes at the wharf yesterday were a fitting climax to the exceptional interest which has been shown in the players chosen for the notable tour. Thousands of people were present to cheer the All Blacks on to their great undertaking, and they cheered and cheered again with great heartiness. To those cheers the All Blacks responded at the call of their manager, Mr. S. S. Deau.

The reception each member of the team received as he embarked, the continuous show of enthusiasm while waiting for the signal for departure, the great display of streamers, and then the hand-waving and final cheers as the *Remuera* moved out, made up one of the most enthusiastic farewells that has ever been accorded to any team. It was a great send-off. In those closing scenes the manager and the captain of the team expressed appreciation of the goodwill shown towards the team. They indicated again that they realised the importance of the task ahead of them. They were confident of upholding New Zealand's great name on and off the field, and to that end would do their best.

Strict attention is to be given during the voyage to exercises, massage, instructional courses, etc., that will, it is hoped make the team quite fitted for the big tour by the time they reach headquarters. The *Remuera* will proceed to Plymouth, via Panama, and a call will be made at Pitcairn Island if the weather is suitable. It is expected that the All Blacks will land at Plymouth on the 2nd September, and that will give them eleven days at Home prior to taking to the field for their first match, set down to be played against Devon on the 13th September.

The Nelson Evening Mail

Departure of the All Blacks
30th July

United Press Association, Wellington, this day

On the tick of 4 o'clock the *Remuera* left the wharf yesterday with the All Blacks on board. Thousands had congregated inside and outside the barriers and cheered each man as he went on board, his name being officially announced as he appeared. The team all wore hats with black bands bearing a silver fern leaf in front. The usual display of streamers floated over the side of the ship, and what was unusual was the inclusion of a number of broad black ribbons in honour of the New Zealand colours. The weather had been showery all day but cleared up just before the *Remuera* left.

The Franklin Times

"All's Well" in Good Fettle
All Blacks' Message
4th August

(Per Press Association, Wellington, this day)

A radio message from the *Remuera* 1,400 miles away says that all is well on board. The All Blacks are in good fettle and have settled down to steady training.

1925

A LETTER FROM PITCAIRN

The following is a brief extract from a letter written by Pitcairn Islander Lincoln Clark to a friend in the United States. Lincoln moved to Pitcairn in 1909 with his 15 year old son Roy, who was later to become well known as the Island's school teacher, and later, postmaster.

2ND MARCH

"… the *Remuera* came day before yesterday, and 'Father' Cameron stopped his steamer from 5 o'clock p.m. until 10 p.m. The *Remuera* is about the only steamer that gives me a good time. The purser, storekeeper and the steward are my very good friends. We all got together in the purser's room and I smoked more cigarettes than were good for me, and drank a few cups of coffee, got ashore about 11:30 …"

1925

PITCAIRN ISLAND
AN INTERESTING NARRATIVE
23RD MARCH

The Thames Star

Written by the Rev. R. Raine
for the *Evening Star*

Pitcairn Island was the only piece of land seen by passengers travelling on the *Remuera* between Wellington and Panama. It is situated in mid-Pacific, about half way between Wellington and Panama. The distance between Pitcairn and Panama is 3520 miles. There is a story of romance associated with this island and its people.

The captain of our ship, Captain Cameron, gave us a lecture on Pitcairn Island a day or two before reaching the place. As is the custom of these islanders, the whole population (consisting of about 180 people) was aroused by our arrival, and quickly gathered from the plantations fruits of various kinds, chiefly bananas and oranges, and other articles for barter or for sale. Boatloads of islanders were soon on our ship's deck, and they did a great trade. It was estimated that in about three hours they must have taken well over £100.

It is a very disappointing thing to these folk if a ship comes within sight of the island and the captain thinks it not worth while to stop, particularly if they have loaded their boats and made ready for doing good trade. Some thirty of our ship's passengers boarded their little boats, and were soon landed on the island itself. It was a delightful day, but the heat was too intense to be comfortable. They returned with an interesting story. I was not a passenger, for there was a big swell, and the tiny boat pitched and rolled too much for my liking.

The natives of the island speak English in rather a broad style. There is music in their voice and music in their nature, for when they finally left our ship they struck up some well-known hymns, one of which was, 'Shall we gather at the river?' and sang them beautifully and with pathos. Some of our ship's passengers confessed to feeling a lump in their throats as they listened to the dying notes of these simple, pure-minded people.

They are a deeply-religious people, and are a standing monument to the effect of the simple Gospel of Christ accepted in its unadulterated condition. Their home is a church. They reverence the Word, they practise family worship, they say grace before and after meals. It was Sunday* when we reached the island, but they did not hesitate to trade. That may, however, be explained by the fact that the islanders are Seventh Day Adventists, hence their Sabbath was on the previous day.

---

*The only previous Sunday call at Pitcairn Island was on 30th March, 1924, approximately a year before the newspaper published this article. Interestingly, the tone of this article is much friendlier towards the Islanders than the report by "T.C.L." (see page 119). Both articles refer to the missionary (Mr Hare) and his wife who were due to stay on the island for six months.

A Seventh Day Adventist minister named Hare left our ship and joined the islanders. I introduced Mr Hare to one of the party, and when Mr Hare said he could only stay six months amongst them one young woman said, with some pathos in her voice, "We would be pleased to keep you always."

There is much that is very primitive about these people. They need to link with their simple goodness the spirit of enterprise and of culture in many respects. Their houses are most primitive – no windows – and the timbers used for building purposes are very rough. Their method of grinding corn is the crude, ancient one. Their garb is rather of a nondescript character. Perhaps just now they may claim to be in the fashion, for their dresses are long. Generally they do not wear boots, but I am told that on festive occasions they do so. Their feet are very broad, and, needless to say, hard and very brown. You cannot say they are of a robust constitution, though in that respect they are medium. Their skin is usually darker than ours. Some have comparatively fair skins, others swarthy, most of them light brown.

Several of the men on the island volunteered to go to the Great War, but none was accepted. They are keen to accept missions. Not long ago one of their leading men boarded a ship which called, and inquired for the Captain. He was directed to the Captain's office, and immediately on entering took from his basket a round bundle parcelled in leaves. This he handed to the captain, with the request that it should be delivered to the Missionary Society of the church to which the islanders belong. The parcel contained £20.

It is the custom of these people to give one-tenth of all their income to God's cause. One-tenth of the product of every orange, pear, banana, or any other tree, and every acre of ground, produce what it may, one-tenth of its product must go to God's cause. If all Christian people were to adopt this principle no church would be very long in debt.

1925

THE ALL BLACKS

4TH APRIL

The Waikato Times.

This newspaper article is reproduced from the *Waikato Times*, New Zealand, with the kind permission of Stuff Limited (https://www.stuff.co.nz), and the National Library of New Zealand (*Papers Past* – https://paperspast.natlib.govt.nz).

Personal Impressions

No more enthusiastic and whole-hearted admirer of the All Blacks, of their play and their demeanour throughout the tour can be found than Mr. B. C. Bennett, of Hawera (says the *Star*), one of the official party, an old footballer, who watched their training from the decks of the *Remuera* and on the fields of Newton Abbot, and their play from the Devon match to the end of the 'journey without defeat,' and was with them in their ordinary life as civilians right to the end of the tour. He therefore had exceptional opportunities of seeing them in every surrounding, and in the light of that experience, to form his own opinion and conclusions.

He says they were a wonderful team, developing in finesse, skill and powers of attack and defence all the time. And he is just as keenly impressed with the personnel of the men as with their play. "They were the finest lot of young men I have ever had the good fortune to know. They wanted no managing," he told a *Star* reporter. "Every man seemed to realise that he was sent to show how New Zealanders play football collectively, and how New Zealanders can behave individually. That they achieved these two objects, there is no shadow of doubt. Their record is ample demonstration. Every man personally looked after his training to keep himself physically fit, and the result was that they were at the top of their form at the end of the tour. The happy relations which early in the tour were set up, was a dominant factor in ensuring good team play. They played as though they were members of a club team, all anxious to win for the honour of their side, but each caring nought who scored as long as the team won. Perfect co-operation and team work were evident throughout. These were ensured because of the happy combination feeling existing the whole time."

Mr. Bennett is emphatic in his admiration for the skipper, Cliff Porter, a fine fellow personally, and a great player. But he says the responsibility of the position seemed to weigh on him with the result that his play deteriorated as the tour progressed. "His unselfishness in acknowledging the fact that Parker, the other rover, was better was beyond praise," said Mr. Bennett, "and showed what a fine sportsman he was. It must have been very hard to urge his own exclusion from the Team in the test matches. Yet Porter stood down willingly because he considered the interests of the team demanded that decision."

Of the reception given to the team wherever they played, much has been written, and that is ancient history. But it was amplified by the Hawera member of the party. He said that from the time of their arrival at Plymouth when the Lord Mayor bade them an enthusiastic welcome to England – in fact, before that, for the Pitcairn Islanders loaded the team with fruit and decorated every member with flowers – right along their progress over England, Wales and Ireland, through

France and Canada, it was one long line of welcomes such as did the heart good to see and hear, and made them proud to be New Zealanders and Britishers. No doubt it helped materially in their resolution to uphold the honour of the Dominion, on the field and off, and was a factor in their record.

Mr. Bennett considers that, speaking generally, a fine type of men play Rugby in those countries of the Old World, and that the matches were popular was shown by the record gates at the matches. "But," he added "it is extraordinary how conservative they are in their methods. The great outstanding difference between the play of the two continents lies in the straight running of the New Zealanders, as compared with the cross the field tactics of the Home teams. And, although there are plenty of good men at Home, fine runners and clever players, they did not seem at the end of the tour to have adopted the tactics of their opponents. It is to be hoped that for the sake of the game some imitation will be done later."

A brief mention only of the Brownlie incident* was made by Mr. Bennett, and he is convinced, as were so many thousands of disinterested spectators, that a sorry mistake was made by the referee. He said he could not understand how it came about because the referee had acted in several other matches, and was selected by them out of four whose names were submitted.

Emphasising, in conclusion, the results and the value of the tour, Mr. Bennett said that every player seemed imbued with the idea that they had come to play football, but, besides the honour of the game, they had to maintain that of the Dominion and of the Empire. This feeling left no doubt in his mind, he said, that it was a great factor in their success, and went a long way to make what was so aptly called by Sir Pember Reeves in his ode written at the presentation of the Loving Cup, a 'journey without defeat.'

---

*Cyril Brownlie became the first man, apparently very unfortunately, to be sent off in a Test Match.

1926-7

IMPROMPTU OCEAN RACE
6TH JANUARY

𝕸𝖆𝖓𝖆𝖜𝖆𝖙𝖚 𝕰𝖇𝖊𝖓𝖎𝖓𝖌 𝕾𝖙𝖆𝖓𝖉𝖆𝖗𝖉.

This newspaper article is reproduced from the *Manawatu Evening Standard*, New Zealand, with the kind permission of Stuff Limited (https://www.stuff.co.nz), and the National Library of New Zealand (*Papers Past* – https://paperspast.natlib.govt.nz).

England to New Zealand
Oil Burner Will Win

(By Telegraph – Special to *Standard*. Auckland, Jan. 5.)

An impromptu ocean race from England to New Zealand between Shaw Saville and Albion liner *Corinthic* and the New Zealand Shipping Company's liner *Remuera* will end next Monday, both vessels having reported by wireless that they will reach Wellington that morning.

Each has on board a large number of passengers as well as cargo. The *Corinthic*, which is a coal-burner, cleared Southampton on December 3rd and the *Remuera*, which uses oil fuel, sailed the following day. In consequence the *Remuera* will win the race of 11,000 miles by one day.*

It is most unusual for two steamers to be despatched from an English port for the same port in New Zealand within such a short period.

The *Remuera* won the 11,000 mile race from England to New Zealand

---

*Despite the fact that this voyage developed into a race, both the *Corinthic* (on 30th December) and the *Remuera* (on 31st December) made stops at Pitcairn Island.

1927

SAD TIMES IN THE OLD COUNTRY
19TH JANUARY

The Thames Star

This newspaper article is reproduced from the *Thames Star*, New Zealand, with the kind permission of Stuff Limited (https://www.stuff.co.nz), and the National Library of New Zealand (*Papers Past* – https://paperspast.natlib.govt.nz).

Immigrants' Stories
Glad to get to N.Z.

Bringing pessimistic stories of the conditions now ruling at Home, immigrants from Scotland and the North of England arrived by the *Remuera*.

They made no secret of the fact that they were glad to get away from the Old Country. It held no promise for them, they said. It was a dull place to live in, and though many of them had received no encouragement to emigrate to New Zealand, and though they had been told that unemployment was prevalent in the Dominion, they had decided, after due consideration, that it was better to come to New Zealand and take a chance than to remain at Home with its pessimism, its workless thousands, and its generally unsatisfactory living conditions.

No False Impressions

"We were not given any false impressions as to our chances of obtaining employment here," said one man on the boat. "We were told, rather, that we would find work hard to get. We have come here knowing full well what to expect. We will have to look for work. We know that. We were told by the authorities before we sailed."

He said that no encouragement was given to other than farmers to emigrate, that the High Commissioner's Office made it plain that men were wanted on the land, but that, as far as the positions in the towns were concerned, more men were available than were required, but things were so bad in England and Scotland that they were glad to get away.

For the Land

Most of the men for the towns had come out on the chance of finding employment; most of those for the country had been nominated and had positions awaiting them on the land.

"Things are very bad at Home," one immigrant said. "It's a good place to be out of. They had settled the strike just before we left. But that didn't improve matters noticeably. It was estimated that 200,000 men previously employed in the mines would remain out of work. That was due to the fact that the mines would not be re-opening until extensive repairs had been effected."

Speaking of the cabled reports that a very busy Christmas had been experienced by the shops in the Old Country, another immigrant said that when they left early in December business was decidedly slack, and there appeared to be no immediate prospects of an improvement.

Not Too Bright

"I am quite sure that as far as the working people were concerned, things were not too bright, and they would not keep the shops very busy," he said. "Conditions at Home are bad. Everything was at a standstill when we left."

It was stated that there was a big boom in motor-buses in Scotland now, and that trams were being scrapped in favour of the more modern means of transport; motor tyres had recently been reduced in price by 20 per cent., and petrol by a penny a gallon.

When the *Remuera* left Southampton on December 3rd last, there were 416 immigrants aboard; when she arrived at Wellington that number had increased by one – James Arthur Pitcairn Twin.

He was called James, after Captain James Cameron, skipper of the vessel; Arthur, after the ship's doctor; and Pitcairn, after Pitcairn Island, because he was born shortly after the vessel left that island. He was born on New Year's Day.

Some Inducement

One man, an engineer, bound for Invercargill, said that before he left he was informed that there was no demand for engineers in New Zealand, although it was stated by the authorities that there was some inducement for plumbers, mechanics and electricians to emigrate.

When the *Remuera* left Home much of the unemployment prevailing was due to the fact that various steel construction works being carried out by local bodies, both in England and in Scotland, were held up because of the fact that steel was not available with which to carry on, and the bodies concerned refused to import material for the works.

1929

GIRL INJURED AT PITCAIRN ISLAND

2ND JANUARY

𝔗𝔥𝔢 𝕳𝖆𝖜𝖊𝖗𝖆 𝔖𝔱𝔞𝔯
and South Taranaki Gazette

This newspaper article is reproduced from the *Hawera Star*, New Zealand, with the kind permission of Stuff Limited (https://www.stuff.co.nz), and the National Library of New Zealand (*Papers Past* – https://paperspast.natlib.govt.nz).

Officers of the steamer *Remuera*, which arrived at Wellington yesterday from Home, reports that when the vessel was at Pitcairn Island the assistance of the ship's surgeon was sought to attend one of the island girls, who had fallen fifty feet from a cocoanut tree. The ship's surgeon, Dr G. E. Wood, landed and attended to the girl, who had been severely injured by the accident, which had occurred twelve days previously.

1929

RETIREMENT OF CAPTAIN JAMES JOHN CAMERON

After 34 years' service with the New Zealand Shipping Company, Captain James John Cameron retired in 1929 at the age of 60. His sea service was much longer than 34 years, however, as he was one of the older generation of seamen who received his early nautical training in clipper sailing ships.

He joined the New Zealand Shipping Company as a junior officer in 1895, and just 12 years later, was promoted to a command.

Captain Cameron had charge of five of the company's steamers before his appointment to the *Remuera*, which he commanded for 23 voyages.

James Cameron was born in Glasgow in 1869. In April 1906, he married Winifred Isabel Whitson in Dunedin, New Zealand. They had one child, a daughter named Isabel, who sadly died at the age of two. They retired to Barnes in Surrey, England. Captain Cameron died in 1947, and his wife, Winifred, died aged 93 in 1973, in Dunedin, having returned to New Zealand, on the S.S. *Rangitata* in 1950 following the death of her husband.

Winifred and James Cameron

GIVE A KODAK.

A KODAK is always sure of a welcome from young and old alike. Get that Kodak now.

AUTOGRAPHIC KODAKS from 27s 6d
BROWNIE CAMERAS from 10s 6d

J. H. WALKER

CHEMIST AND PHOTOGRAPHIC
DEALER,
OPP. RAILWAY STATION.

Newspaper advertisement from 1927

The Photographers
OF PITCAIRN AND THE PANAMA CANAL

Many of the photographs in this book were taken by three men, Henry Keyse, David Aldersley, and Peter Zerface. Henry and Peter were hairdressers, working for the New Zealand Shipping Company, and David was a professional photographer living in New Zealand.

The next few pages have a short biography of the three, together with their portraits, drawn for me by my friend, the late artist and stamp designer, Jennifer Toombs.

Henry Keyes was the one who first got me interested in the subject matter of this book. I collected a few of his real photo postcards, and determined to find out his full name as he only gave his initials on the front of most of his photographs, 'HGK'. It was a difficult search, and at one time I hired a geanealogy specialist, but eventually I found him on a crew listing for a voyage of the *Remuera*, and that was a very exciting day!

David Aldersley was my next interest. He had been credited by one American researcher as the photographer of most of the postcards in this book, but that is not the case, it was only that he reproduced them for sale, using his own style of postcard back, and sometimes adding his 'A' code to the front for identification purposes. David was a renowned photographer in his own right, taking many wonderful views of New Zealand for his own postcard business, but he only travelled by the New Zealand Shipping Company once, and that was in 1895 when he emigrated to New Zealand from the UK on the *Rimutaka*.

Peter Zerface photographed many similar subjects to Henry Keyse. In the second edition of the book, *The Romance of Pitcairn Island*, Peter is credited for some of the photographs included in its pages.

Many of the early photographs and postcards are uncredited, and could have been taken by any of the above three photographers. It is a very difficult area to research given the number of years that have passed.

Henry George Keyse

TIMELINE

1879: Born in Ross on Wye, Herefordshire, UK

1901: Listed as a hairdresser, age 21, on the Census at his sister's house together with a boarder, Charles Wilandt, age 25, also a hairdresser

1905-6: SS *Tongariro*, steward/barber

A Pitcairn Islander, possibly Andrew Young, wearing clothes donated by the Shipping Company, photographed by Henry Keyse in the early 1920s

1907-8: SS *Paparoa*, steward/barber

1909: SS *Warrimoo*, barber

1909-1910: SS *Rimutaka*, barber

1911-1912: SS *Turakina*, barber

1913-1916: SS *Remuera*, barber

1913: Met his wife to be, Violet Eleanor Bennett White, when she was travelling to New Zealand on the *Remuera*

1914: Photograph of an iceberg in the South Pacific is the earliest photograph I have seen which is credited to 'HGK'

1914: Married Violet White in New Zealand

1916: Working as a barber on the *Remuera* during her first call at Pitcairn (24th October)

1917-18: SS *Hurunui*, second steward. In 1918 the *Hurunui* was torpedoed and sunk by U-boat 94, 48 miles south-west of the Lizard

1919: SS *Kent*, second steward

1919-1929: SS *Remuera*, barber

1921: Age 42, birth of his daughter, Stella, in Croydon, UK

1928: SS *Berengaria*, steward

1931-1945: SS *Rangitata*, barber

1967: Died in Worthing, West Sussex, UK, aged 87

In 1924, Lincoln Clark wrote from Pitcairn Island:
The barber from the steamer Remuera *came ashore to take a few pictures. The one taken at the boat house at the landing will show a few, at least about 12, of the grown male population.*

Before the Panama Canal opened, the *Remuera* often passed quite close to icebergs in the Pacific. This is one of many photographed by Henry Keyse

Another Henry Keyse photograph of the journey through the Panama Canal

David James Aldersley

TIMELINE

1862: Born in Keighly, Yorkshire, UK

1884: Managed the family china business and shop in Yorkshire while taking up an interest in photography

1895: Emigrated on 22nd August, with his wife and four children, to New Zealand on the SS *Rimutaka*, arriving in Wellington on 8th October. Lost no time in setting up his business as a photographer

c.1900: Moved to 561 High Street, Lower Hutt (in the Wellington region of New Zealand), in a house named Ingleboro. The house, once isolated, is still standing today and much enclosed by more recent buildings

c.1905: Started a postcard business, and from about 1907, began numbering his cards on the front as the 'A' series

1928: Died in New Zealand, aged 66

This montage style postcard was very popular at the time. It was created and re-photographed by David Aldersley containing five photographs which were probably taken by the two New Zealand Shipping Company hairdressers, Henry Keyse and Peter Zerface

It is my opinion that the majority of David Aldersley's real-photo postcards were published from his own photographs. However, as I have not been able to find any records of him travelling by ship after his 1895 voyage on the *Rimutaka*, 20 years before the Panama Canal was opened, I must assume that all photographs taken on Pitcairn and in the Canal, were by other people and then published by David Aldersley on their behalf.

Two postcard views of Wellington with steam ships in the harbour. There is an interesting advertisement on the building, lower left, which reads, "Take a Kodak with you". David Aldersley's postcards are very popular with collectors, and often come up for sale on eBay at high prices.

Peter Philip Zerface

TIMELINE

1881: Born in Chelsea, London, UK

1901: Listed under his original surname, Zerfahs, as a hairdresser, and a boarder in a house in Leyton, age 19, on the Census of that year

1903: SS *Tongariro*, barber and steward. Peter's older brother John Frederick Zerface was also on board, working as a Baker's mate

1903-1906: SS *Turakina*, barber and steward

Three generations of Pitcairn Island men photographed on board the *Ruahine* in 1916. This photograph, taken by Peter Zerface, also appears in the book *The Romance of Pitcairn Island*, by W. Y. Fullerton

1906: SS *Rimutaka*, steward

1912-1929: SS *Ruahine*, barber

1913: Age 32, married Amy Neva Clinch at Picton, New Zealand

1916: Working as a barber on board the *Ruahine* during her first call at Pitcairn Island (26th November). Several people went ashore, and many islanders visited the ship and received presents

1930-1940: SS *Rangitane*, barber

1940: Age 59, working as a barber on board the *Rangitane*. The ship was sunk by the Germans after the crew and passengers had left in lifeboats. The illustration of Peter, drawn by Jennifer Toombs, is based on his appearance in a Pathé News film showing the rescued survivors of the *Rangitane*

1948: Died in Nelson, New Zealand, age 66

I would love to find out if Peter Zerface and Henry Keyse knew each other. They worked for the same company but never, as far as I know, voyaged together (even though there were sometimes two barbers on

NZSC ships). They both worked on the SS *Tongariro* in the early part of their careers, but in different years. They both had photographs published by David Aldersley. They both worked through the First and Second World Wars. They both met the Pitcairners. They both photographed the Panama Canal and sold their postcards to passengers.

A rough sea photographed by Peter Zerface from the deck of the *Ruahine*.
See also his photographs on page 41 and 74

The writing style on Peter Zerface's photographs is very similar to David Aldersley's, which leads me to believe that Aldersley was the publisher

been sick yet so I make a better sailor than I thought with love from I Smart

S.S. Remuera
At Sea
Oct 21 -05

Dear Maggie

I will now take the pleasure of writing to you, I expect you were begining to think we had forgotten you both but we are having such a grand time with three fellows we made friends with on the boat train we really car'nt settle down to write, the shipping company had to put us all up at different hotels at plymouth as the boat did'nt come down from London till Mon: so the three fellows taken us to the Palace on Sat night + they are looking after us on the boat, we all sit together at the table for our meals + we do see life, we got on the boat about 5.30 on Mon: but we did'nt sail till 8 o'clock, we both felt a bit dicky the first day we were on the boat but we feel in the pink now + I must tell you we havn't

An interesting message on this old *Remuera* postcard

Rhymes en route

A PASSENGER'S POEMS

Although at least one these poems was written before the 1920s, I think they are a rather nice way to end this look at the life and times of the *Remuera* and her passengers.

I can't be certain that the poems are out of copyright, but according to the State Library of Victoria, Australia, which holds a printed copy, they would classify them as orphan works (whereby the copyright owner is unknown and untraceable).

The initials W.A.O. appear at the end of the final poem, so perhaps he or she was one of the passengers on that late 1916 voyage?

I hope you enjoy them, and that they transport you back to a different time and place.

R.M.S. "REMUERA." New Zealand Shipping Co.
11,900 Tons.

ON DECK

To help me write my song,
I walk the deck along,
   Observing and reflecting,
Till sounds the evening gong.

I hear the rigging rattle,
I hear the children prattle,
   And from the cushioned deck-chairs
The flow of tittle-tattle.

And often, as I've tarried,
I've heard soft voices carried
   From shady nooks that shelter
The flirting of the married.

METRICAL EXPERIMENTS

An artist that lived at Colon
One morning got up before dawn,
    And sketched, *a la* Phil May,
    The wonderful Spillway,
Before he had anything on.

There was a young girl of Port Said,
Whose voice could awaken the dead
    When she sang, every mummy
    Turned round on its tummy,
And finally stood on its head.

WHAT MADE ME BILIOUS?

Was it the ham
And the subsequent jam?

Was it the roast,
Or the well-buttered toast?

Was it the curry
I ate in a hurry?

Maybe the salad
Was the cause of this ballad!

Can a lamb's fry
Give you spots in your eye?

Can over-much bread
Make you wake with a head,

Or a helping of fowl
Make you look like an owl?

Can biscuits and cheese
Weaken your knees?

Can squeak and some bubble
Make you see double?

O doctor, please doctor, don't look supercilious,
But tell with professional candour punctilious,
The reason I'm feeling so horribly bilious.

(Doctor, *sotto voce*)

Mag. sulph. and a war-ration diet, the silly ass!

R.M.S. REMUERA

WEST INDIES, DECEMBER, 1916

Our lamps are faintly glowing,
  The moon shines bright with liquid light
On water swiftly flowing
  Beneath the tropic night.
The engines' rhythmic ringing,
Its diapason flinging,
Says loud to all – Good fortune fall
    Upon the *Remuera*!
Says loud to all – Good fortune fall
    Upon the *Remuera*!

And from afar appearing,
  Some light awhile on lonely isle
Will guide our steady steering,
  And beckon mile on mile.
And on the bridge, unsleeping,
The watch, its vigil keeping,
Our doubts dispel – we know all's well
    On board the *Remuera*,
Our doubts dispel – we know all's well
    On board the *Remuera*,
            W.A.O.

MAY I ASK A FAVOUR?

Thank you for reading this book. If you enjoyed it, found it useful or otherwise, then it would be great if you could take a moment to leave a review on Amazon. It doesn't need to be a long review, a sentence is fine, and will make me very happy!

Printed in Great Britain
by Amazon

34547184R00096